# LEGAL SECRETS
## for
# INDEPENDENT FILMMAKERS

# LEGAL SECRETS
# for
# INDEPENDENT FILMMAKERS

## AKUA BOYENNE
Attorney-at-Law

Cosmopolitan Publishing
Beverly Hills, California

Cosmopolitan Publishing
Beverly Hills, California

Nothing in this book is to be considered as the rendering of legal advice, either generally or in connection with any specific issue or case. Readers are responsible for obtaining advice from their own attorney or other professionals. This book and any agreements herein are intended for educational and informational purposes only.

Printed in the United States of America
ISBN: 978-0-615-67453-7

*Book Design by Jennifer Omner, ALLPublications.com*
*Edited by Kimon Koufogiannis*

## Dedication

To my parents, William and Lenita, for being an inexhaustible source of love and inspiration throughout my life. Dad, your intelligence and compassion and, Mom, your strength and beauty will always transcend time and space for all those who were touched by your unforgettable presence.

# Ithaca

When you set out on your journey to Ithaca,
pray that the road is long,
full of adventure, full of knowledge.
The Lestrygonians and the Cyclops,
the angry Poseidon — do not fear them:
You will never find such as these on your path,
if your thoughts remain lofty, if a fine
emotion touches your spirit and your body.
The Lestrygonians and the Cyclops,
the fierce Poseidon you will never encounter,
if you do not carry them within your soul,
if your soul does not set them up before you.

Pray that the road is long.
That the summer mornings are many, when,
with such pleasure, with such joy
you will enter ports seen for the first time;
stop at Phoenician markets,
and purchase fine merchandise,
mother-of-pearl and coral, amber and ebony,
and sensual perfumes of all kinds,
as many sensual perfumes as you can;
visit many Egyptian cities,
to learn and learn from scholars.

Always keep Ithaca in your mind.
To arrive there is your ultimate goal.
But do not hurry the voyage at all.
It is better to let it last for many years;
and to anchor at the island when you are old,
rich with all you have gained on the way,
not expecting that Ithaca will offer you riches.
Ithaca has given you the beautiful voyage.
Without her you would have never set out on the road.
She has nothing more to give you.

And if you find her poor, Ithaca has not deceived you.
Wise as you have become, with so much experience,
you must already have understood what Ithacas mean.

*Constantine P. Cavafy (1911)*

# CONTENTS

# Acknowledgments

It deeply stirs my soul when I reflect on all those who have made this book possible. Thanks to my colleagues and friends, Cornell and Eric, for their tireless effort in preparation of this book.

And a special thanks to my fiancé, Allen, for his love and support.

# Introduction

How many times have you had a legal question about the business side of your career and wished you had a trusted friend that could help you so you could concentrate on what you do best, the creative side of your career? Fortunately, you now have this book derived from many years of legal experience and expertise. The intention of this book is to educate you about basic legal principles and to empower you to intelligently discuss entertainment related business matters. I truly believe an educated client is an empowered client.

This book is about you and your career. It is about your mastering the basic legal principles so you can go out into the world with confidence and take control of situations, whether you are socializing at networking events, participating in development meetings, putting your production team together, interacting with wealthy investors, or, setting the stage for your attorney to ultimately negotiate the most successful deal possible.

Each chapter in this book will guide you simply and effectively through fundamental legal and business matters at every stage of filmmaking, including: acquiring a property, organizing your business, negotiating production agreements, obtaining financing or seeking distribution.

Every chapter contains key negotiation tips and legal secrets of the business side of filmmaking. Most chapters are furnished with examples of legal agreements stripped down to some of their major deal points. The agreements only touch on some of the major issues dealing with the complicated world of independent filmmaking. There are many other important issues that are not covered that will directly impact your deal. When reviewing entertainment agree-ments, it is in your best interest to seek legal advice since one sen-tence or even on word can significantly change the whole deal.

Key negotiating tips and legal secrets are all highlighted in grey. Consider the highlighted part as your trusted friend whispering the answers to your questions in your ear. And although it does not replace the eventual need to hire an entertainment attorney, this indispensable manual is designed to help you learn how to clearly articulate your most basic needs so that your legal representative can negotiate the best deal possible on your behalf.

# CHAPTER 1

## OBTAINING LITERARY PROPERTY

The Option Purchase Agreement is one of the most important legal documents associated with film production. In general, an option is the right to purchase property (i.e. the screenplay, book, magazine article, etc.) in the future based on certain terms and conditions. Think of it as dating. A Producer is interested in the screenplay, book or magazine article a Writer has to offer but isn't entirely sure yet whether he'll be able to fully commit to it. It all depends on certain terms and conditions, including the purchase price. In the meantime, he'd like to lock it down. So he acquires *the right* to buy the desired property in the future.

Why is that important? In order for a Producer to ever have a chance to transform someone else's property into the next big hit, the Producer must first obtain written permission from the copyright owner, the author or creator of the property to make the film. This is where the option purchase contract comes into play. Without explicit permission, the Producer may find it impossible to secure, among other things, financing and distribution.

This binding legal document addresses everything you need to have initially covered including compensation, credit, and future rights where the underlying literary property is concerned. This chapter will highlight its most important aspects so that both Producers and Writers know what to expect.

It usually starts the same way. A Producer hears about or reads a book or screenplay ("literary property") and falls head over heels for it. He simply has to turn it into a movie. Next thing you know, the lucky Writer is being asked out to lunch. "I'd like to make a movie out of your book (or screenplay)," confesses the love struck Producer. "I'd be honored," the delighted scribe concurs. At the back of his mind, the Producer should already be thinking how to get his date to sign an Option Purchase Agreement in order to secure the rights to develop the property. On the other hand, the Writer should be concerned about the length of time he's willing to accord the Producer to develop his work as well as the credit, compensation and other major deal points.

Of course, no matter how many butterflies any Producer experiences in his or her stomach, they will still want you to sign an option purchase agreement (sort of like a pre-nup). And rightfully so, the reason why they want to purchase the rights to the property *in the future* is to give themselves enough time to develop the project without incurring huge costs up front.

In this context, develop means arranging for financing, attaching talent (i.e. director, actors, etc.) and rewriting the screenplay. Smart Producers rarely pay the entire purchase price to acquire those rights before they have arranged for financing and know they're able to successfully develop the project.

The Option Purchase Agreement gives the Producer the exclusive right to control the property. Once the deal points are agreed upon, those terms and conditions constitute the option purchase contract.

Let's take a closer look at a simplified version of an option and purchase agreement so you become more familiar with its major deal points.

# OPTION AND PURCHASE AGREEMENT
## (Completed Script)

**THIS AGREEMENT**, effective as of _____, 20\_, is made by and between _____ [name of producer] located at _____ (the "Producer") and _____ [name of writer] located at _____ (the "Writer"), concerning the rights to a _____ [e.g., book, screenplay, play, magazine article] entitled "_____" and the materials upon which it is based (the "Property"). The following terms and conditions shall apply:

---

**Introductory paragraph.** This paragraph should not be taken lightly because it contains the effective date, which may subsequently control some of the terms of the contract. Since the parties rarely sign the agreement on the same day, it is important to establish the date right at the top rather than running the risk of having two different dates next to the signatory lines at the end of the contract.

The introductory paragraph introduces both parties (and mailing addresses) to the contract — namely, the Producer and the Writer. It distinguishes the type of literary property being optioned and provides the title of the work.

---

1. **OPTION FEE and OPTION PERIOD**: In consideration of the mutual promises contained herein, and the payment to Writer of $_____ (the "Option Fee"), Writer hereby grants to Producer the exclusive, irrevocable right and option (the "Option") for _____ months (the "Option Period") to acquire the exclusive motion picture, television, videocassette, and all subsidiary, allied and ancillary rights in and to the Property pursuant to the terms set forth below.

**Option Fee.** The first deal point to negotiate is the option fee, which determines how much money the Producer initially pays the Writer. This is different from the actual purchase price. It's simply paying for the option to buy the rights to the property at a specific time in the future.

There is no standard amount paid as an option fee. Many independent films are free whereas studio deals can range anywhere between $5,000 to as high as $100,000 just for the option itself. Needless to say, if you're a producer, you want to keep the fee as low as possible.

**\*Legal Secret\*** In an effort to avoid high fees, a nice way for Producers to put it to Writers is: "I'm not in the business of paying for options, I'm in the business of making movies and I want to make your movie." Always accentuate the positive.

**\*Legal Secret\*** In order to strengthen your position (or weaken the other party), always keep in mind the following factors that can influence the option fee: the demand for the property (which can result in a bidding war), the heat the Writer has generated (if, for example, they're sitting on a bestseller), the relationship between the Writer and the Producer (a pre-existing relationship usually dictates a lower fee), the Producer's resources (if the Writer feels the Producer has a good chance of making the movie, a lower option fee can be negotiated) and the actual length of the option period (generally speaking, the lower the fee, the shorter the option.)

**Option Period.** The option period is the length of time the Producer has to develop the project by arrange financing, attaching talent, rewriting the script and deciding whether to actually purchase the rights.

Although this deal point is negotiable, the usual range is between 12–18 months.

> Producers prefer the option period to be as long as possible so that they have enough time to attach talent and arrange financing.
>
> Writers, on the other hand, want a shorter option period to avoid tying up their property. If the Producer ends up dragging their feet, the Writer would like to be able to option it to another Producer.

2. **EXTENSION OF OPTION**: Producer shall have the right to extend the Option Period for one (1) period of twelve (12) months for $_____ non-applicable to the Purchase Price. For the right to the extension of the first Option Period there must be one of the following:

(a) Letter of commitment to direct from an established director;

(b) The project is set up at a company, major studio or mini-major studio able to fund the project;

(c) Substantial negotiations in progress for complete financing of the film; or

(d) Letter of commitment to act in the film from one star.

> **Extension of Option:** So what happens if the Producer begins to run out of time, you ask? We've all been there. It happens. If only there was a little more time, you'd be able to bring the project to fruition.
>
> This is where the "extension of option" comes to the rescue. It affords the Producer an additional amount of time to develop the project.
>
> Notice the clause clearly states, "Producer shall have the right to extend the option." It's the *Producer's* exclusive right. If this clause has been included in the contract, only the Producer has the choice of extending the time required to develop the project.
>
> The usual extension accorded is the same as the initial term (or may be less). During the initial negotiation, the Producer may push for a number of extensions.

How does all this exactly work? Let's imagine we're nearing the end of the initial term (12 months – 18 months) and although our Producer is getting close to securing financing or attaching a director or star to the project, he isn't quite there yet. At that point, the Producer gives the Writer written notice to extend the option period and depending on the terms of the contract, can either: pay the Writer an additional flat payment; or base the extension upon the fulfillment of certain conditions.

Most Producers prefer to pay a flat fee and be done with it. If the option was free to begin with, they might be willing to subsequently offer $250 – 2500 for the extension.

Writers, of course, would love a higher fee, although smart Writers will negotiate to keep the extension contingent upon specific milestones being reached. It's the best way for a Writer to be able to gauge whether his Producer is on top of his game or merely dragging his feet.

3. **EXERCISE OF OPTION**: Producer may exercise this Option at any time during the Option Period, as it may be extended, by giving written notice of such exercise to Writer and delivery to Writer of the minimum Purchase Price as set forth below. In the event Producer does not exercise said Option during the period as it may be extended, this Agreement shall be of no further force or effect whatsoever and all rights granted hereunder remain property of Writer.

**Exercise of Option:** This is where dreams start becoming reality. It's about the Producer's right to purchase and subsequently own the exclusive rights to the underlying property.

If the Producer has an option without the right to purchase the rights, the option is worthless. It would only allow him to haggle with the Writer at a later date. With the Producer unable to purchase the option, the Writer could simply walk away when the option expires or even attempt to drive up the purchase price.

Producers "exercise the option" by giving written notice and paying the purchase price.

4. **PURCHASE PRICE**: The Purchase Price for the Granted Rights will be 2% of the direct cost budget (i.e. excluding bond and financing fees, contingency, and interest) ("Budget") of the first theatrical motion picture produced hereunder with a minimum payment of $80,000 and a maximum payment of $200,000.

---

**Purchase Price:** This is the amount the Producer pays the Writer in order to acquire the rights to the property. It's a happy time. Up to this point the Producer has only optioned the right to purchase the property (these two have only been dating). Now, the Producer is certain he wants to purchase the property (now there's a commitment — sort of like getting married).

The purchase price itself can be: 1) a flat fee; 2) a percentage of the film's budget; 3) or both.

Most Producers pay up to 2.5% of the budget. However, the Producer will add a "ceiling" which is the highest amount he's willing to pay out in case of a significant budget increase and the Writer will often negotiate a "floor," meaning the lowest amount he's willing to accept.

---

**\*Legal Secret\* "Direct Cost Budget"** This is a very important consideration, which deserves special mention. Here is where a couple of missing words from the contract can end up being a very costly mistake. If you read the aforementioned clause carefully, you'll realize it refers to 2% of the "direct cost" budget rather than simply the "budget". Depending on how the film is financed, it is imperative the Producer limits the Writer's percentage to the "direct cost budget" as opposed to the "budget" itself since the former excludes bonding, contingency, financing fees and interest.

Once again, it is vital to apply the 2% to the "direct cost budget" rather than the total budget. For example, let's assume you have a budget of 10M out of which only 7M is your direct cost budget. If it's not specified that the purchase price applies to the "direct cost budget," the Producer may end up overpaying the Writer $60,000.

## 5. CONTINGENT COMPENSATION:

(a) Net Proceeds. Writer shall be entitled to receive an amount equal to Five Percent (5%) of One Hundred Percent (100%) of the "Producer's Net Proceeds," if any, derived from the Picture.

(b) Performance Bonus. In addition, subject to distributor's approval, Writer shall be entitled to box office bonuses of Fifty Thousand Dollars ($50,000) when the domestic theatrical box office receipts as referred to in *Daily Variety* equal One Hundred Million Dollars ($100,000,000), an additional Fifty Thousand Dollars ($50,000) when the domestic theatrical box office receipts as referred to in *Daily Variety* equal One Hundred Fifty Million Dollars ($150,000,000), and an additional Fifty Thousand Dollars ($50,000) when the domestic theatrical box office receipts as referred to in *Daily Variety* equals Two Hundred Million Dollars ($200,000,000).

---

**Contingent Compensation.** Contingent Compensation is a general term used to describe an additional payment based upon the happening of a certain event including the following:

**Net Proceeds.** If the film makes Net Proceeds, the Producer, generally will grant the Writer a net profit participation of 5% Net Proceeds for sole writing credit, reducible to 2.5% for shared writing credit. Therefore, if the film makes net proceeds, then the Writer will share a percentage of the profits. Net Proceeds refers to the remaining amount of profit after all the costs and expenses are paid.

**Let's take the film *Slumdog Millionaire* as an example:**
   1.   The production budget = $15M

---

2. Distribution by Fox Searchlight so let's estimate a marketing and distribution fee of $25M
3. That's $40M in costs
4. The film grossed 140M domestically
5. 50% goes to theaters, so $70M to Fox Searchlight
6. That's a net of $30M ($70M minus $40M in costs)
7. If the writer negotiated a 5% share in "Net Proceeds," that's 5% of 30M
8. 5% of $30M = $1.5M

**Writers, if you fail to negotiate to include this clause, it is a $1.5M mistake**

**\*Legal Secret\*** The presence of a single word in Net Proceeds clause can make a huge difference. Which word? You've guessed it — "Producer." There is a world of difference between: 100% of "Net Proceeds" which means a percentage of the whole pie, and 100% of "Producer's Net Proceeds" which, in effect, means only half.

Producers, if you fail to add the word "Producer" to your "Net Proceeds," you will be obligated to share the whole pie. For you, it can mean the difference between the Writer pocketing $1.5M instead of only $750K. Enough said.

**Performance bonus:** This is another form of contingent compensation that is based on box office performance. If the picture generates a particular level of theatrical box office gross receipts, the writer earns an additional bonus:
1. If box office is 100M = $50,000
2. If box office is 150M = $50,000
3. If box office is 200M = $50,000

So, in the example of *Slumdog Millionaire*, how much money did the Writer make in box office bonuses? Once again, enough said.

## 6. CREDITS:

(a) In the event a motion picture based substantially on the Property is produced hereunder, Writer shall receive credit in the following form:

Examples for Book Authors

Based on the book by _____

Examples for Screenplay writers

Written by _____

Written by _____ & _____

Written by _____ and _____

(b) Provided that Writer is not in material default hereof, Writer will receive the following credit on a single card on screen and in paid ads controlled by Producer and in which any other writer or producer is accorded credit and in size of type (as to height, width, thickness and boldness) equal to the largest size of type in which any other writer or producer is accorded credit.

(c) No casual or inadvertent failure to comply with credit requirements hereunder shall be deemed a breach of this Agreement.

---

**Credits.** If the writer is a member of the WGA, the writer's credit will be determined in accordance with the WGA Agreement. In general, the WGA Agreement requires the credit to appear in the main titles, on a separate card, in a size equal to the director and producer credit and requires that the credit appears in paid advertisements.

If the writer is not a member of the WGA, the Writer must be conscious of negotiating every detail when it comes to credit. Most of the time, Producers will use the WGA guidelines anyway since it is the industry standard.

Example for Book Authors:

"Based on the book by_____"

- Denotes the Author of a book

Example for Screenplay writers:

"Written by_____"

- Denotes the Writer is responsible for coming
  up with the story (the basic plot) as well as
  writing the actual screenplay

**\*Legal Secret\***

"Written by_____ & _____"

- Denotes a team of writers working together

Whereas, "Written by_____ and _____"

- Denotes writers who have worked individually,
  usually referring to a rewrite

**The Writer should negotiate for:**

1. Placement
   a.   On screen credit
   b.   On a single card
   c.   In the main titles

2. Paid Advertising
   a.   The Writer should make sure to have
        his credit included in all paid advertising
        such as billboards, one sheets, etc. or
        wherever the Director's or Producer's
        own credits appear
   b.   It's worth noting the Writer should try
        to tie his credit to the Director since the
        DGA has very strict rules.

3. Size of Credit — the Writer's credit should be the same
        size and type as that of the Producer or Director

**7. GRANT OF RIGHTS**: Effective upon Producer's exercise of the Option, Writer does hereby exclusively sell, grant, and assign to Producer, all rights in and to the Property not reserved by Writer, throughout the universe, in perpetuity, in any and all media, whether now existing or hereafter invented, including, but not limited to, the following: all motion picture rights, all television rights, all rights to make motion picture versions or adaptations of the Property, to make remakes and sequels to and new versions or adaptations of the Property or any part thereof.

> **Grant of Rights:** This designates what the Producer actually purchases. For example, he may purchase all rights to the property or just limited rights such as film and television rights.
>
> A smart Producer, however, is after the acquisition of all rights. This paragraph is all-inclusive and therefore it places the burden on the Writer to reserve specific rights.

**8. RESERVED RIGHTS**: All publication rights, including audio-book rights, are reserved to Writer for Writer's use and disposition, including but not limited to the right to publish and distribute printed versions of the Property and author-written sequels thereof (owned or controlled by Writer) in "book form, whether hardcover or softcover, and in magazines or other periodicals, comics or coloring books . . . "

> **Reserved Rights.** These are the rights the Writer will attempt to reserve (i.e. retain).
>
> Writers often seek to reserve:
> 1. Print publication — book or magazine (subject to holdback)
> 2. Live stage — a play (cannot be televised)
> 3. Radio — reading of a play
>
> For the majority of scripts, there are no reserved rights.

9. **ARBITRATION:** Any claim, controversy or dispute arising hereunder shall be settled pursuant to California law by arbitration before a single arbitrator in accordance with the rules of the Independent film & Television Alliance (IFTA) held in Los Angeles, California. The award of the arbitrator shall be binding upon the parties and judgment there may be entered in any court. The prevailing party shall be entitled to all arbitration costs and reasonable attorney fees.

> **Arbitration:** This is an especially important clause, if you are an independent Producer. You should always add an arbitration clause to the contract. If the parties involved are unable to resolve a dispute on their own, this is the fastest and cheapest way to have it settled. I strongly recommend using IFTA since all of their arbitrators are attorneys who specialize in independent film.

10. **PREMIERES, DVDs**: Producer shall invite Writer and one (1) guest to all celebrity premieres in the United States and to screenings at major festivals within the United States and Canada. In addition, provided that Writer is not in breach of any warranties and representations hereunder, Producer shall provide Writer with one (1) DVD of each production produced hereunder in which Writer receives credit at such time, if ever, as DVDs of such production become generally commercially available.

If the foregoing meets with your approval, please so indicate by signing in the space provided below.

> **Premieres, DVDs:** Writers should not expect to be automatically invited to the premieres and receive DVDs of the film. Writers

must ask for them. Also, Writers should ask to be reimbursed for expenses incurred while attending the premiere. On the other hand, Producers may invite the Writer only to North America premieres and festivals to limit the expenses.

Very Truly Yours,

(PRODUCER'S COMPANY NAME)

By:_____

An Authorized Signer

Agreed to and accepted:

_____

(WRITER)

# CHAPTER 2

## ORGANIZING YOUR BUSINESS

As an independent filmmaker entertaining a new project, you're about to set out on your own personal "journey to Ithaca". And although you should always wish that "the road is long, full of adventure, full of knowledge", you need to make sure you build first a solid foundation or you won't be able to last the planned journey. Without proper organization, the trials and tribulations ahead will eventually win you over and prevent you from ever reaching the land of your dreams.

### SOLE PROPRIETORSHIP

Many independent filmmakers start out as a sole proprietorship without even knowing it. You may not realize it but that's what you already are, if you've decided to travel solo on this journey. A sole proprietorship is defined as a business that is operated by an individual who has not formed a separate legal entity such as a corporation, limited liability partnership or Limited Liability Company (LLC). The sole proprietorship becomes your default business structure as soon as you take your first all-important steps to making your film, like shopping your script, taking meetings or negotiating deals. It is what you are automatically, if you do nothing to form a separate business entity.

If you're in the beginning stage and planning on being the only one aboard your vessel, it may be a wise move to operate as a sole proprietor. It will make your steerage simple and keep it inexpensive. In California, there is no minimum annual tax or use tax charged to sole proprietors. You do not need to file a separate tax return for your business. Attaching Schedule C to the individual income tax return will suffice since that's what discloses business revenues and expenses. No legal formalities are required, and there are no legal fees or significant expenses incurred. You will just need to register your company with the state if you are doing business under a fictitious name (also known as "DBA" Doing Business As) or any name other than your personal name.

> **Legal Secret** When selecting a name for your DBA, consider choosing the title of your film. For example, "Me and Mrs. Jones" is better than simply your own name, Bill Jones. The benefit is two-fold. From a legal perspective, you simplify the process of converting your DBA into an LLC when the time comes since it leaves no room for confusion to anyone with whom you're already doing business. Also, in the eyes of the world, you appear to be operating as a professional film business.

## FICTITIOUS BUSINESS NAME

It's not as difficult as you might think to establish a fictitious name ("DBA"). The first step is to go online to the County Clerk's office and download the forms. Once you have them filled out, you are required by state law to publish a legal notice in a local newspaper within 30 days of filing your new name. That's about it. You're all set to carry on with your journey. Now, you can legally open a bank account and every transaction suddenly becomes an opportunity to develop critical name recognition for your product. Just remember, for accounting purposes, to keep your business records separate from your personal. If your film acquires financing, all expenses can be recouped and you will have organized records for tax purposes.

Many filmmakers remain a sole proprietorship when entering preproduction armed only with a script or if they're planning on shooting a short film with a small cast and crew and no investors.

What happens though if you realize you're actually going to need a bigger boat and you start hiring employees to aid you on your upcoming crossing? When your company increases in size, a different kind of legal structure becomes necessary, first and foremost, because you want to be able to individually protect yourself and your employees from liability claims. The biggest drawback to operating as a sole proprietorship is that, if anything goes wrong on the set or off the set related to the film, you'll be personally liable. For example, you send your assistant out to deliver your script to a potential actor but they're involved in an accident along the way? You could be held liable for compensating the injured party and, if you end up losing the lawsuit, the injured party has a right to take away from you not only your business but all personal assets too. That's right. And that may include your home and personal bank accounts. You'll be setting out on a perilous voyage only to end up with nothing.

Another reason why filmmakers form a legal structure is to secure investors to finance the film. It is dangerous to raise funds otherwise. If a potential investor gives money to a sole proprietorship, it may transform the relationship into a partnership, which means your newly minted investor becomes personally liable for any business obligations, as well. Understandably, no investor wants to run that risk. One way to protect yourself from such a calamity is by forming a limited liability company (LLC).

## LIMITED LIABILITY COMPANIES

Congratulations! With your employees and investors on board, you've decided to create a limited Liability Company ("LLC"). The LLC is a blend of partnerships and corporations. It provides limited liability for the owners and investors of the LLC like a corporation, but the LLC is treated like a partnership for tax purposes. You get to enjoy the best of both worlds. Liability protection, on one hand, and favorable tax treatment, on the other. In other words, you're almost ready to launch your boat.

An additional feature about an LLC is that you will still get to be your own captain since there are no formal governance rules. You will be able to guide your outfit whichever way you think best because, unlike corporations, there are no mandatory board meetings or mandatory shareholder accounting. In a business where "time is money," this flexibility is priceless.

Of course, it's never sunny all the time. The biggest drawback of using an LLC is they are subject to state income tax. In many states, the tax is modest and no tax is assessed until there is a total income of $250,000 or more per year. However, in California, LLCs are subject to an annual tax of $800 irrespective of whether you make a profit or not.

---

**\*Legal Secret\*** Forming an LLC is more straightforward than it may sound. The first thing you need to do, in most states, is file the Articles of Organization (Form LLC-1) with the Secretary of State which establishes legal recognition of your entity. Don't let the name scare you. The Articles of Organization is but a simple one-page form, which actually comes with very helpful instructions. To obtain the form, go online to the Secretary of State website, fill it out, download it and mail it to the Secretary of State of the state in which the film company will be located. See? Simple.

---

That's not the end of the story and the next step is a little trickier because every film production company must also have an Operating Agreement. Although the Articles of Organization are relatively easy to fill out, a well-drafted Operating Agreement can prove challenging. Don't worry though. Help is on the way. Your entertainment attorney is there to expertly put it together for you. The time for embarking on your great adventure draws nearer still!

Why is the drafting of this legal document so important? You may be the sole master of your ship but there will still be a need for order. Your Operating Agreement establishes the rules for managing and operating your film business. It structures the terms of the understanding among the owners of the LLC (the filmmakers). It spells out who will have creative control and who's in charge of the business decisions, how money will be distributed, how the LLC will be terminated, and so on and so forth. As far as the investors, in particular, are concerned, the Operating Agreement is a vital tool as it clearly delineates the nature of their equity interest in the film and shields them from personal liability.

One size doesn't fit all though when it comes to Operating Agreements. Each film's finance plan is different. One has to be custom made for a film production company's individual financing strategy. Some film companies will restrict the initial return on investment to the investors first before paying back any other unpaid "hard cost." Others may opt to restrict additional capital into the LLC to avoid diluting the original investors' investment interest. It's alright. No two ships have ever been commandeered alike. The most important thing is everyone understands the deal.

What follows is a simplified version of an Operating Agreement to help familiarize you with some of its major points so you can intelligently deal with your investors as well as pave the way for your entertainment attorney and accountant to execute the necessary transition from a sole proprietorship (or partnership) to an LLC. A treasure trove of negotiating tips and secrets are also unearthed to ensure the smoothest sailing possible for everyone you've invited on board. Ship ahoy, Captain!

## OPERATING AGREEMENT

**OPERATING AGREEMENT for _____, LLC**

**THE SECURITIES REPRESENTED BY THIS AGREEMENT HAVE NOT BEEN REGISTERED UNDER THE SECURITIES ACT OF 1933, ("SECURITIES ACT") NOR REGISTERED UNDER ANY STATE SECURITIES LAWS.**

A.  This Operating Agreement is entered into as of _____ by and among the "Managing Members" and the "Investment Members" (whom hereinafter may be referred to individually as a "Member" or collectively as "Members") as further defined below.

B.  The Members desire to form a _____ limited liability company (the "Company") for the purposes set forth in Paragraph 2.5.

C.  The Members enter into this Agreement to form and to provide for the governance of the Company and the conduct of its business, and to specify their relative rights and obligations.

NOW, THEREFORE, the Parties agree as follows:

---

The first line designates the name of your LLC, which ideally should be the title of your film.

The bold print deals with Securities laws. Generally speaking, if your investors aren't active (hands-on) investors and are instead passive investors, you will be required to publicly register the investment agreement with the government on a federal and state level unless you use an exemption. The public

---

registration is in place as a means of monitoring filmmakers and protecting potential investors from being defrauded.

**\*Legal Secret\*** Low budget films must always seek to find an exemption, as it is prohibitively expensive as well as time consuming to file documents with the government. One way to avoid triggering the SEC is to only work with accredited ("wealthy") investors.

(In our example, we are assuming our investors to be passive and accredited so working within an exemption and with no need to register the transaction with the government.)

## ARTICLE I: DEFINITIONS

Capitalized terms used in this Agreement have the meanings specified in this Article or elsewhere in this Agreement; and, when not so defined, shall have the meanings set forth in the Act.

1.1 "Investment Members" means all members of the Company making monetary Capital Contributions to the Company, aside from the Managing Members.

1.2 "Managing Members" means _____ (the producer) and _____ (partner). The Managing Members may be referred to herein as "Managers."

1.3 "Picture" means the feature length motion picture currently titled, "_____" produced by [_____, LLC] and directed by _____ to which Company intends to produce and control all rights. A copy of the business plan for the Picture is attached hereto as EXHIBIT A.

**Definitions.** The first article of the Agreement distinguishes between the "Investment Members" (your actual investors) and the "Managing Members" (that means you, the Producer, along with your partners). It also establishes the title of the Picture, the name of your production company and that of the Director.

**\*Legal Secret\*** You will find the business plan referred to in the last sentence attached at the end of this chapter as Exhibit A. If your film falls in the micro budget category or all your investors are friends and family or pre-existing business people, a business plan may not even be necessary. Most low budget Producers prefer to avoid having to draft and pay for a business plan.

## ARTICLE II: ORGANIZATIONAL MATTERS

2.1    The Managers have caused organizing documents in the form of the ARTICLES OF ORGANIZATION attached to this Agreement as EXHIBIT B, to be filed with the Secretary of State.

2.2    The name of the Company shall be _____, LLC.

2.3    The principal executive office of the Company shall be _____, or such other place or places as may be determined by the Manager from time to time.

2.4    The registered agent for service of process on the Company shall be _____, whose address is _____. Managers from time to time may change the Company's agent for service of process.

2.5 The business of the Company shall be to produce and control the rights to the Picture and to perform and conduct any other activity necessary or incidental to the foregoing or in the opinion of the Managers in furtherance of the objects of the business of the Company.

2.6 The name and address of the Managing Members are as follows:

_____

_____

2.7 The name and address of the Investment Members are attached hereto as EXHIBIT C.

---

**Organizational Article.** It deals with the fundamentals of organizing your LLC including:

1. The Articles of Organization is the formal document to be filed with the state.
2. The name of your LLC.
3. The location of your LLC.
4. The registered agent who's the person responsible for receiving all legal notices. Most filmmakers use their entertainment attorney in that capacity.
5. The principal purpose of the company which is to finance, produce and distribute a motion picture.
6. It also lists the names and addresses of all Members.

---

## ARTICLE III: CAPITAL AND CAPITAL CONTRIBUTIONS

3.1 The Managers shall contribute as their Capital Contribution services to the Company, including, but not limited to, producing and directing the Picture and other such services.

3.2  Investment Members' Capital Contribution shall be as outlined on EXHIBIT C.

3.3  The Company's total capitalization will not exceed $_____.00 The current budget for the Picture is attached hereto as EXHIBIT D.

---

**Capital and Capital Contributions.** This clause determines individual contributions. Managers (Producers) provide all film-related services while Investors provide the money.

**\*Legal Secret\*** The last section deals with capitalization. Here, there's a cap on the budget to protect the investor from having their investment diluted. This section provides your investor with assurance that their equity interest will not be reduced lower than a given percentage.

---

## ARTICLE IV: ALLOCATIONS

4.1  The allocation of Revenue shall be as follows:

4.1.1  First, a reasonable amount of the Company's income shall be used for operating, production and exploitation expenses, and outstanding obligations directly related to the production and exploitation of the Picture, if any, to the extent such amounts are not included in the Budget of the Picture;

4.1.2  Second, each Investment Member shall recoup 120% of his/her Capital Contribution on a pro rata basis;

4.1.3  Third, the Company shall satisfy any outstanding

obligations of the Company in connection with the Picture, including deferred payments incurred in connection with the Picture;

4.1.4 Next:

4.1.4.1 50% shall be paid out to Investment Members on a pro rata basis determined by the amount of each Investment Members' Capital Contribution;

4.1.4.2 Simultaneously, 50% shall be paid out equally to the Managers (i.e., 50/50);

---

**"Allocation" of revenue.** It deals with what position you're in when money starts coming in.

Investors expect to recoup their investment with a premium anywhere between 10–20% and, in case the film turns out to be a hit, an additional bonus on the "back end." This is how it usually plays out:

1.  The filmmaker raises sufficient funds for the pre-production, production and post-production stages of the movie (the "Budget") from various investors ("Investors.")
2.  Let's assume the best-case scenario of the movie actually getting made, becoming a blockbuster and, ultimately, profitable.
3.  Income from all sources (e.g. box office revenues, DVD sales, VOD, license fees from TV stations, etc.) gets paid out as follows:
    a.  First up, even before the Producer, are the Distributors of the film who deduct their fees and costs off the top of all distribution revenue known as "Gross Receipts."
    b.  The Gross Receipts minus the distribution fees

---

and costs are the actual monies that reach the Producer.

c. He then has to make good on any items contained in the Budget that have not been met yet.

d. Next, the Producer repays his Investors the full amount of their contribution along with a 20% premium on a pro rata basis.

**\*Legal Secret\*** The Latin phrase "Pro rata" implies that all Investors will be paid at the same time in direct proportion to the amount of money they invested. The less common words "Pari Parsu", on the other hand, mean all investors are paid "in equal step" or just "equally" regardless of their investment.

e. Afterwards, all deferments are paid.

f. Lastly, the Net Proceeds are split between the Producers and his Investors who receive "back-end" compensation on a pro rata basis out of the "Investor's Share". That typically consists of 50% of the total Net Proceeds, the other 50% going to the Producer as his "Producer's Share". Any talent and other non-investor third parties who were promised a back-end share in the movie also have their percentage taken out of the "Producer's Share."

## ARTICLE V: MANAGEMENT

5.1    The Company shall be managed by the Managers.

5.2    All decisions about, regarding or otherwise pertaining to the creative and business aspects of the Picture, including, but not limited to, the production, distribution and exploitation of the Picture shall be made mutually by the Managers.

5.3 Investment Members shall not have say over any aspects regarding the Picture, including but not limited to all, artistic production elements in connection with the production of the Picture, and all commitments and contracts relative to any of the foregoing.

---

**Management.** It deals with who has business and creative control. This clause is extremely important since it clearly takes the investor out of the "active investor" category and precludes them from having the right to make any demands or suggestions down the line regarding any aspects of the Picture including cast, locations or credits even though they're its principal funders.

**\*Legal Secret\*** If a single Investor contributes a substantial percentage of the budget, he may demand and should be accorded an Executive Producer credit.

---

## ARTICLE VI: RISK FACTORS

Investment in the film industry is highly speculative and inherently risky. There can be no assurance of the economic success of any motion picture since the revenues derived from the production and distribution of a motion picture depend primarily upon its acceptance by the public, which cannot be predicted. The commercial success of a motion picture also depends upon the quality and acceptance of other competing films released into the marketplace at or near the same time, general economic factors and other tangible and intangible factors, all of which can change and cannot be predicted with certainty.

---

**Risk Factors.** This is another crucial article since it clearly warns investors of the high-risk nature of the venture they're about to

---

> participate in. Both state and federal law dictate full disclosure of all inherent risks.
>
> **\*Legal Secret\*** Even if registration is not required, the anti-fraud provisions of the securities laws require that you make full disclosure of all facts that a "reasonably prudent investor" would need to know in deciding whether to invest. If all your investors are accredited investors, use the operating agreement to provide full disclosure.

## ARTICLE VII: ACCOUNTS AND ACCOUNTING

Complete books of account of the Company's business, in which each Company transaction shall be fully and accurately entered, shall be kept at the principal business office, or at such other locations as the Manager may determine from time to time, and shall be open to inspection and copying on reasonable Notice by any Member or the Member's authorized representatives during normal business hours, but no more than once per calendar year. The costs of such inspection and copying shall be borne solely by the Member individually and in no way shall be considered to increase Members' Capital Contribution.

> **Accounts and Accounting.** It deals with the how and where your books are kept and when they're available for review in case of an audit.

## ARTICLE VIII: MEMBERSHIP MEETINGS AND VOTING

8.1    There shall be two classes of membership, Investment Members and Managing Members. No Investment Member shall have any rights or preferences in addition to or different from those possessed by any other Investment Member.

8.2 The Managing Members shall maintain controlling interest in the Company and make all decisions regarding the Company and the Picture.

8.3 Members may participate in a meeting through use of conference telephone or similar communications equipment, provided that all Members participating in such meeting can hear one another. Such participation shall be deemed attendance at the meeting.

> **Meetings and Voting.** It safeguards the equal rights of all Investors. There is no such thing as VIP status. At the same time, it specifies that the Producers have final say on all aspects of the film. It also identifies the best method for members to attend meetings, even by phone.

## ARTICLE IX: DISSOLUTION AND WINDING UP

10.1 The Company shall be dissolved upon the first to occur of the following events:

10.1.1 The expiration or termination of the Company's rights and interest to the Picture;

10.1.2 The expiration of the Term of Existence of the Company;

10.1.3 The sale of all or substantially all of the assets of Company;

10.1.4 Upon the vote of Members holding the majority of the interest in the Company;

10.1.5 The happening of any event that makes it unlawful or impossible to carry on the business of the Company; or

10.1.6 Entry of a decree of judicial dissolution.

10.2. On the dissolution of the Company, the Company shall engage in no further business other than that necessary to wind up the business and affairs of the Company. The Managers shall wind up the affairs of the Company.

> **Dissolution and Winding Up.** It lists all eventualities that can automatically terminate an LLC.

## ARTICLE X

10.1 ARBITRATION: All disputes arising out of this Agreement shall be submitted to arbitration in accordance with the rules of the Independent Film and Television Alliance before a single arbitrator. The prevailing party shall be entitled to reasonable attorneys' fees and costs. The arbitrator's award shall be final, and judgment may be entered upon it by any court having jurisdiction thereof.

> **Arbitration.** This is an especially important clause, if you are an independent Producer. You should always add an arbitration clause to the contract. If the parties involved are unable to resolve a dispute on their own, this is the fastest and cheapest way to have it settled, bypassing the need for a lengthy legal dispute and its accompanying astronomical costs. I strongly recommend using IFTA since all of their arbitrators are attorneys who specialize in independent film.

IN WITNESS WHEREOF, the parties have executed or caused to be executed this Agreement on the day and year first above written.

**MANAGING MEMBERS:**          **INVESTMENT MEMBERS**:


_____          _____


_____          _____

# EXHIBIT A
# BUSINESS PLAN

**What goes in a Film Business Plan?**

It highlights the creative elements of the project, demonstrates the business strategy and offers a realistic projection of how much revenue the film is expected to generate. It should include the following:

1.  Two-page Executive Summary for prospective investors who may subsequently request the full plan.
2.  Biographies of all principals including producers, director, writers, actors or other attachments.
3.  One-page Screenplay synopsis.
4.  Comparable box office performance sheets by films of similar budget and genre.
5.  Overview of the current state of the film industry.
6.  Risks Factors
7.  Film Production plan including locations and unions, if any.
8.  Budget summary.
9.  Distribution plan including the film's marketing strategy and target audiences.
10. Finance plan detailing the sources of the film's funding.
11. Financial projections showing how investors will be able to recoup their contribution.

# EXHIBIT B
# ARTICLES OF ORGANIZATION

**\*Legal Secret\***

If you don't mind a little effort, it's possible to file the Articles of Organization on your own. You are required to file this document with the State in order to establish legal recognition of the LLC. It's a one-page form and comes along with very helpful instructions. To obtain the form go on line to the Secretary of State website, fill it out, down load it and mail it to the Secretary of State in the state in which the film company will be located.

# EXHIBIT C
# INVESTMENT MEMBERS

| Name and Address | Capital Contribution | Percentage Interest |
|---|---|---|
|  |  |  |
|  |  |  |

# EXHIBIT D
# BUDGET

# CHAPTER 3

## FINANCING INDEPENDENT FILMS

This chapter is designed to give you a broad understanding of how independent feature films are funded. It is essential that filmmakers have a solid Financing Plan in place before starting to raise financing for the film. Since every film is different you must explore the various avenues of film financing and determine which ones are appropriate for your film. We will start by looking at Equity Finance and discuss the laws and documents related to investor financing. Next, we will explore State Tax Incentives and explore the difference between tax credits and cash rebates. Then we will look at the elements you need in place to take advantage of Presales and how to monetize Presales. And finally, we will discuss when to use and how to maximize your Crowd Funding campaign.

---

## EQUITY FINANCE: INVESTOR FINANCE DEALS

Many independent films are financed by investors whether they are friends and family or complete strangers. When an investor offers you money in exchange for an interest in your film business, that interest is referred to as "security" and you are entering the field of securities law.

There are a number of ways to structure an investor finance deal (also known as an "equity investment") including using a corporation, limited partnership or LLC. In every instance, the securities laws are in place to protect the investors. Some producers have been known in the past to create a lot of misleading hype about their film and all the name stars supposedly starring in it, so the federal and state governments passed laws to safeguard against such fraudulent deals. Since investors rarely play an active role in film production, these laws attempt to regulate filmmakers by forcing them to disclose all pertinent information in advance and preventing them from offering any misleading information.

The federal agency in charge of regulating securities is called the Securities and Exchange Commission ("SEC"). In order to regulate each transaction, it is required that all securities are registered with the state and federal government. For maximum protection, the person running the business (the filmmaker) is obligated to register the offering (investment deal) with the SEC as well as with every state in which his investors reside.

Virtually every independent filmmaker, however, avoids registration as the cost to register is prohibitive (upwards of $50,000) and the process itself highly complicated. To be able to do that, they must qualify for one or more of the statutory exemptions, which are generally restricted to what's called "private placements" as, oppose to filing with the government as a "public offering."

Exemptions allow filmmakers to bypass the SEC when offering and selling their securities although there are tight restrictions placed on these types of investment interests including no public advertising, no general solicitation of investors and a required pre-existing relationship between filmmaker and investor. Albeit, the current administration is in the process of relaxing these restrictive laws regarding private placements (see JOBS Act).

## STATUTORY EXEMPTIONS

The filmmaker who wishes to avoid registration with the SEC must use at least one of several exemptions, the most common of which are:

**Intrastate Offerings**. In order to be able to qualify, your film production company has to be formed in the selected state, a significant amount of business to occur within its boundaries and all investors to reside in it.

> **\*Legal Secret\*** This is one exemption that's really risky since the protection it affords can be lost even if only one of your investors resides out of state. If you're no longer exempt, you automatically become subject to personal liability claims, which open the door to all of your investors being able to sue you if anything goes wrong.

**Accredited Investor Exemption.** The federal law exempts transactions that are limited to accredited investors when the total offering price is less than 5M. The most typical types of accredited investors include: 1) individuals with income in excess of $200,000 ($300,000 with spouse) in each of the two most recent years; or 2) an individual or joint with spouse whose net worth (excluding primary residence) exceeds $1,000,000 at the time of the investment purchase.

Since all regulations are in place for the protection of the investors' interest, the law assumes that accredited investors who already enjoy a substantial income can afford to take a financial risk and possess the necessary business acumen to evaluate the risks and merits of an investment. As such, the SEC is willing to forgo registration and its accompanying lengthy formal disclosure requirements.

> **\*Legal Secret\*** Only for accredited investors, use the LLC's operating agreement as a disclosure document so you avoid paying extra legal fees to draft a Private Placement Memorandum (PPM).

**Rule 506.** Under Rule 506, a filmmaker is allowed to raise money from an unlimited number of accredited investors (income above

$200,000 or net worth more than $1,000,000) and up to 35 non-accredited investors (income below $200,000 or net worth less than $1,000,000). The major difference between the Accredited Investor Exemption and Rule 506 is the non-accredited investors MUST be given disclosure documents similar to those used in registered public offerings (SEC).

---

**\*Legal Secret\*** For non-accredited investors, use the Private Placement Memorandum (PPM) and subscription agreement rather than the operating agreement as a disclosure document. You must determine whether your investors are accredited or non-accredited. If you have even one unaccredited investor you need a PPM. You can have up to 35 non-accredited investors. If all your investors are accredited and you have a pre-existing relationship with them then you do not need a PPM. You can just use an LLC and operating agreement as your disclosure document.

---

## PRIVATE PLACEMENT MEMORANDUM ("PPM")

If you raise money from at least one accredited investor (and you don't know them, that is, you do not have a "pre-existing relationship" with them), you must use a Private Placement Memorandum ("PPM") as your disclosure document. Nevertheless, the current presidential administration is in the process of relaxing the restrictive measures imposed by the "pre-existing relationship" rule (See JOBS Act).

A film PPM is a legal document that provides full disclosure of all the terms and conditions of an offer to sell interest in a movie to an investor. It provides such detailed information in order to protect investors from fraudulent transactions. It includes the business plan and any marketing materials used to solicit interest in the investment. It is the safest way to raise money because it reduces the risk of being sued by investors in case the film fails. Since it discloses all the risks of a film investment, it makes it hard for investors to later claim they were not adequately warned.

## LIMITED LIABILITY COMPANY ("LLC") and OPERATING AGREEMENT

If you raise money only from accredited investors with whom you have a "pre-existing relationship," you don't need an expensive and time-consuming PPM. Instead, you can form an LLC using an Operating Agreement.

The Operating Agreement is the key component of any LLC. It's a legal binding contract between you and your investors which affords the filmmaker creative and business control, states that your investors will invest money, details each investor's individual contribution, and presents a clear picture of the order in which profits from the film will be paid out.

The Operating Agreement can also serve as the disclosure document you need to submit to your accredited investors. Under federal and state law, a company that's formed with the express purpose of raising money for a project must generally provide full disclosure of all material facts pertaining to the proposed investment and its inherent risks so that a "reasonably prudent investor" can make an informed decision. All Operating Agreements should include a "Risk Factors" paragraph that clearly advises potential investors that an independent feature film constitutes a high-risk venture.

Once again, the rules and regulations governing full disclosure are so extensive in order to protect potential investors from fraud, but equally, if not more important, to safeguard you, the filmmaker, against any later claims by those same investors that they were misled.

Filmmakers should not attempt to draft or negotiate the terms of an agreement without the aid of an experienced entertainment attorney. If you're not fully aware of the rules, you are only setting yourself up for possible litigation and, if anything goes wrong, investors can end up suing you for all their money back and, potentially, even fraud.

## ACTIVE INVESTORS

> **\*Legal Secret\*** One way to avoid public registration, drafting a PPM or even forming an LLC, is to turn your investors in what is called "active investors."

An active investor is regularly involved in helping you, the filmmaker, make important decisions with respect to your film. Their contributions may range in all aspects of film production including script selection, rewrites, choosing a director and casting the lead actors, selecting the line producer and director of photography, problem solving during production, mapping of financing and distribution strategies, and so on and so forth. Obviously, this type of deal can only be limited to a few investors. It would be difficult to complete a film with too many cooks in the kitchen so to speak. Your active investors need to be relatively experienced in matters of the film industry to be able to add value to your project and have a hands-on approach on a regular basis.

In case of active investors, you can simply use a business plan combined with an appropriate investment vehicle (e.g. a financing agreement, joint venture agreement, initial corporation or an LLC) to provide them with all necessary information to make an informed decision.

## FILM BUSINESS PLAN

Once again, all you need to have with active investors is a solid business plan coupled with the appropriate investment vehicle such as a financing agreement, joint venture agreement, initial corporation or an LLC. Active investors run no danger of triggering the SEC since it is considered a non-security transaction and are only a small active group involved in every stage of the film process.

> **\*Legal Insight\*** You should carefully phrase your business plan so that it doesn't imply an intention of raising money from more than a few active investors because, from a certain point onwards, it becomes impossible to keep a large number of investors "actively" involved in a business venture in any meaningful way. As a result, you will lose your active investor's status and be required to file with the SEC or find a suitable exemption.

## What goes in a Film Business Plan?

The film business plan is not a binding contract; it is simply a marketing tool. It should include your budget, the bios of your creative team, a short synopsis of the screenplay, a casting list, your distribution plan and a record of box office grosses of comparable films —both hits and misses. A list of Risk Factors is also necessary to provide potential investors with full disclosure of the high-risk nature of their venture.

---

# TAX INCENTIVES

## PRODUCTION INCENTIVES

The phenomenon of "runaway productions" first appeared back in the 1990's. American filmmakers started shooting in foreign countries in order to take advantage of discounts offered to them abroad which significantly helped reduce overall production costs. The term "runaway" refers to the economic migration so to speak of a film (or television) production from one state or country to another.

As a result, many U.S. states began offering their own tax

incentives. They wanted to bring film business back home in the interest of promoting tourism, stimulating the local economy and creating jobs within their borders. And it worked.

Tax Incentives are essentially free money with the total payout varying from state to state. As a responsible filmmaker, you should be scouting filming locations which offer you this advantage. In this section, we will look at the various types of state and federal tax incentives, examine cash rebates and tax credits, review how to monetize tax credits, and finally, learn how to use state and federal tax incentives to attract investors.

## CASH REBATE/ TAX CREDITS

The most common production incentives are cash rebates and tax credits. In some states, they may also take the form of exemptions from taxes on sales, hotel and lodging or fuel and electricity. They are generally calculated based on the total amount of expenditure incurred within the state including both labor, and equipment and supplies costs.

## CASH REBATE

A few states have programs where production companies receive direct rebates based on the amount of qualifying expenditures or jobs created within their jurisdiction. These funds do not require a tax return to be filed.

For example, at the end of shooting a $1 million film in Mississippi, you submit copies of your accounting records and receipts to the Mississippi Film Commission and they will send you a check for 25% of all qualifying expenditures (a rebate of $250,000). It usually takes 3–6 months after production is finished and all expense receipts have been submitted for the producer to receive the check from the state. Some producers put this money toward post-production, others use it as an immediate return to their investors.

## TAX CREDITS

Tax credits can be either refundable or non-refundable as well as transferable or non-transferable.

## REFUNDABLE TAX CREDITS

A refundable tax credit functions in much the same way as a production rebate with the main difference being that it's administered by the local taxing authority and can only be claimed by filing a tax return. The production company must file a tax return regardless of whether it has any income or owes tax in the jurisdiction. If the production company does owe tax, the Film Commission will deduct the amount of the tax owed and a refund will be granted for the remaining balance.

For example, after completing a $1 million film in New Mexico, you file a tax return and accounting records with the State of New Mexico Film Commission and they will send you a check, minus any taxes owed, for 25% of all qualifying expenditures (or $250,000).

## NON-REFUNDABLE, TRANSFERABLE TAX CREDITS

A non-refundable (no money back) tax credit may be transferable. A transferable tax credit is one that may be sold or assigned to a local taxpayer. This transfer can be handled directly by the production company or indirectly through the use of a broker who will charge a commission. And the production company will need to discount the credit from its face value to entice local taxpayers to purchase them.

For example, you plan to shoot a $1 million film in Connecticut. Since you will be getting tax credits of 30% upon completion, you get a broker to lend you 80% on the dollar (80% of 30% equals a 24% tax credit) which is $240,000 (minus the broker fees). Now, that money is available to you to make your film as part of your $1 million production budget. This type of tax credit is very popular for independent film producers because it provides them with an important percentage of their budget up front.

## NON-REFUNDABLE, NON-TRANSFERABLE TAX CREDITS

A non-refundable, non-transferable tax credit means you cannot exchange your tax credit for money and you cannot transfer your credit to a local taxpayer. The production company can only use the incentive to offset a current tax liability of the production company. The excess can generally be carried forward and used to reduce taxes in subsequent years. Kansas and California (budgets over 10M) are states with non-refundable and non-transferable credits.

## REBATES VS. CREDITS

Studios and larger independent production companies will generally look first to states that offer rebates before considering states with transferable tax credits. Since cash flow isn't a major issue, they prefer to get 100% of every rebate dollar back as opposed to transferable tax credits which often have to be advanced at as low as 75% of their actual value. That's a twenty-five cent loss on every dollar or a 1M loss for every 4M tax credit. A state's 30% tax credit gets diluted to roughly 23% net to the production whereas a rebate is dollar for dollar.

## INCENTIVES ARE AVAILABLE IN MOST STATES

Many, if not most, US states now offer film incentives. As previously noted, US incentives are generally calculated based on the total expenditures incurred within the state, including both labor, and equipment and supplies costs, and are paid directly to the production entity. Examples of states offering refundable credits are New York and New Mexico. Whereas South Carolina and Florida make rebates available. Non-refundable but transferable credits, which require the producer to sell the credit to an eligible taxpayer in the state, are offered in several states, including Louisiana, Pennsylvania and Connecticut.

> **\*Legal Insight\*** Film incentive programs are ever changing. You must call the state Film Commission office for the very latest update and if you end up using the state incentive program, get it in writing.

## MONETIZING TAX INCENTIVE

Banks or other lenders often monetize refundable tax credits allowing production companies immediate access to funds so that they can pay for current expenses rather than having to wait until after filming is complete. However, an additional fee is generally associated with this type of an advance. Monetization may be the only option for small independent filmmakers since you have to remember your rebate or refundable tax credit don't come through until several months after you submit all necessary documents and receipts to the tax incentive office. Studios and large independent film companies, on the other hand, can afford the luxury of waiting since they have no problem cash flowing their budget.

When a film qualifies under a state's tax credit program, rebates and tax credits can be pre-funded providing the film with enough money to begin principal photography. Even so, most lenders require the majority of your funding to be already in place only utilizing the rebate or tax credit as the final piece of the producer's financing. Unfortunately, many independent filmmakers do not have most of the funding in place so they're unable to ultimately take advantage of this type of financing and resort to using investors. In that case, you provide the investor with a written agreement indicating that although they've loaned you only 85% of the value of the state incentive upfront, they're entitled to the whole amount once the credit or rebate comes in which amounts to a 15% return.

The good news is that you've now succeeded in turning credits into actual money and you can begin shooting your film.

## STATE TAX INCENTIVES USED TO ATTRACT INVESTORS

Small independent film companies can also use their tax incentives as a way of attracting potential investors. The Producer chooses to shoot his film in a state where rebates or transferrable tax credits are available so that he can pass the subsidy on to his investors once it's released by the State.

For example, if a Producer shoots a 1 Million dollar film in New Mexico, the State of New Mexico will issue a 25% tax rebate (approximately $250,000) which can be sold for a little less than face value. That check can then be passed on to the investors considerably minimizing their exposure since they will only be risking an average of 75 cents on the dollar.

> **\*Legal Secret\*** In order to secure financing from a skeptical investor, you can carve the tax credit out of your finance plan and pledge it to them. It will be a much easier sell once they realize they'll be able to recoup a large percentage of their investment within the first year.

## FEDERAL TAX CREDITS—USE TO ATTRACT INVESTORS CODE SECTION 181

The American Jobs Creation Act Of 2004 (the Act) and the 2004 enactment of Section 181 made federal tax incentives available to investors in independent film and television productions within the United States. This tax incentive was generally extended by Congress for either a one or two-year term. At the end of 2011, however, Congress chose not to extend the package so all of its provisions have expired. As of January 2012, *Section 181* is no longer available for financing purposes. Nevertheless, there is a good chance Congress will extend the Act once again in the future and make it retroactive in order to continue to stimulate the economy and prevent runaway productions from taking place.

Section 181 essentially dictates that if you shoot at least 75% of your production (with a budget below $15 million) within the United States, then your investors will be able to deduct 100% of their investment from all passive income of the same year. And if the investor is actively involved in the operation of the production, they may deduct the total amount from all active income earned in the same year. This makes for an extremely attractive proposition to all investors.

For example, if an investor is in the thirty-five (35%) tax bracket and makes a $1 million investment into a qualified production, the actual net investment will be $650,000 since they can take a deduction against that full $1 million against their income. Therefore the value of the deduction is $350,000 (35% of $1M).

## CODE SECTION 199

In addition to the tax reduction incentives under section 181, the income received also has tax opportunities under Code Section 199, which was also added by the same Act. Under the manufacturing sections of the Act, only film (not television) production businesses are considered "manufacturing businesses." As of 2010, manufacturing businesses can deduct an amount equal to 9% from income generated by qualified production activities. The deduction may be limited by the amount of W-2 wages paid. For example, if $100 were received then the taxable income would be $91.

## STATE AND FEDERAL TAX INCENTIVES COMBINED

State rebates and incentives along with Section 181 greatly minimize an investor's risk on what would be otherwise considered a risky venture. By combining the two incentives, you can conservatively reduce their exposure by 50%. Once again, any actual benefits depend on the investor's annual income, their total investment in the movie as well as the filming location.

For example, let's assume a budget of $2M. The Investor invests $1M and their annual income is 5M with 10M in assets. Their annual taxes come up to approximately $1.75 M (35% tax bracket) and there are no other tax write-offs. Under section 181, if they invest $1M dollars, they will be actually risking only $650K while saving approximately $350,000 in federal income taxes.

And that's not all! Suppose the producer chooses to shoot the film in Louisiana, which offers a 30% tax credit on, your gross spend in the state, minus tax rebate broker fees. That's around $300,000. You can pledge that credit to the investors so that they end up getting approximately $650K in combines tax deductions and tax credits from the Federal Government and the State of Louisiana for their $1,000,000 investment in your feature film.

## PRESALES

Another way for a Producer to finance his film is by negotiating a pre-sale deal to foreign territories. Each foreign Distributor signs a contract agreeing to license the rights to the film for that particular country once the film gets made. The Distributor typically pays only a small percentage (10–20%) of the fee up front and the rest upon completion and delivery of the product. The benefit to the Producer is that he can take the presale (distribution) contract and any similar agreements he might have with other foreign Distributors to a bank dealing with entertainment finance and use them as collateral to secure a loan. This is called "banking the paper." When the film is complete, the Producer delivers it to the foreign Distributors and they pay the balance of the licensing fees to the bank plus interest in order to pay off the Producer's loan.

The main reason the foreign Distributor is willing to sign a licensing contract ahead of time is so that he gains an advantage over his competitors who will have to make a higher bid once the film is complete and being sold on the open market.

Before the foreign Distributor even considers a pre-sale, however, the Producer must be able to present him with a solid package containing certain elements already in place, like a marketable director, a known writer, at least two name stars, and also, nowadays, a great sizzle reel. Genre is another key consideration as a foreign buyer is after commercial films which will easily translate in their native country. Action, horror and thriller are the usual suspects as their stories are not heavily reliant on dialogue and are able to transcend cultures.

## PRESALE SCENARIO

In exchange for a 20% commission, the Producer will usually hire a Sales Agent who makes on their behalf all necessary calls, sets up meetings and presents the film to foreign Distributors at film markets.

> **\*Legal Secret\*** Many Producers naturally wonder if they can avoid paying the 20% commission by negotiating the presale deal on their own. The reality is Sales Agents have pre-existing relationships with foreign film Distributors from various countries. That's what you're paying for. They are experienced in each region's language, currency, customs, and laws, and Sales Agents are better placed to be able to collect once your film is released since any local Distributor will want additional product and cannot afford to cheat them.

A Sales Agent becomes your film's biggest advocate in hopes of securing that coveted presale contract. He shows every Distributor he knows your captivating sizzle reel and tirelessly extols the virtues of the Producer's stellar track record, the compelling script, the seasoned director and name actors.

Convinced it's a sure bet, the foreign buyer agrees to license the yet unmade film's rights for his own country by signing a short form agreement reflecting the major deal points with the Sales Agent, and placing a deposit of 10–20% in the Producer's production account with the remaining balance being paid upon completion and delivery of the film.

## MONETIZING PRESALES

The Producer takes the various signed pre-sale contracts to his local bank and negotiates a loan using the contracts as collateral. The bank will also want to make sure the Distributor is financially solvent and likely to still be around when the time comes to pay the remaining licensing fee. Provided they have a solid track record and substantial assets on their balance sheet, the loan will usually be issued against the presale contract. Still, the bank will only lend a percentage of its full face value in order to hedge its bets. For example, if all of the Producer's contracts are worth a total of 1M minus the 10–20% deposit, leaving approximately $800,000, the bank might be willing to lend him $600.000.

The Producer uses the loan to make the film. Once complete, he delivers it to the foreign distributors who have already licensed it. The Distributors, in turn, deposit the balance of their licensing fee to the Producer's bank to pay off the loan. The Bank gets its money plus interest. The Sales Agent gets its commission. The Distributor has the film. And the Producer can make a profit by licensing the film in all the remaining unsold territories.

## PRESALES AS AN INCENTIVE FOR INVESTORS

The key to enticing potential investors is presales and tax incentives. Why are they so important? Think of it this way—if you were to expose your investors to $1M or more of pure equity, there's a likely chance you'd only see a small percentage of that investment to be able to repay them. Since equity remains the most challenging aspect of film financing, you must make sure you come up first with a solid plan. Only after you have solid commitments of a presales and tax credits, should you begin to approach your investors for the remaining amount.

The biggest advantage of using presales as part of your financing plan is that distribution has already been built in the equation. For example, if you're asking investors only for 200K for a 1M movie with presale contracts selling it to foreign markets and tax incentives already in place, you're presenting a much more viable investment opportunity.

## GAP FINANCING

Once the Sales Agent completes their presale deals, some foreign countries will be left unsold. If the Producer requires additional funds to finish the film, the Sales Agent estimates the future value of those territories and a Gap financing company may agree to authorize a loan based on those evaluations. Gap financing can only occur with presales already in place. Before agreeing to supply gap financing, the Gap financing company will carefully review the existing presales and determine from those presales an estimate of the remaining territories. If you sold United Kingdom and France for a certain amount, your financing company can reasonably expect you to sell Germany and Spain for a certain amount. Nevertheless, this remains a high-risk loan since there isn't really any contract to be used as collateral as was the case with presales. The Gap financing company trusts the whole package will come together because of the track records of both the Sales Agent and Producer as well as the commercial value of the film. Gap financing companies are therefore in a position to cover only a small percentage of the budget, usually between 5 and 10%, and at a high interest rate of as much as 25%.

## BOND COMPANIES

In the case of presales, the bank is fully aware the Distributor's commitment to license a film hinges on the film actually being completed. What happens though if the Producer goes over budget and is unable to complete the film? The Distributor isn't obligated to honor his agreement anymore and, as a result, the bank doesn't get its loan repaid.

To safeguard itself against such default, the bank requires the Producer to obtain a completion bond. In this type of insurance, a completion guarantor agrees to put up any money needed to finish the film should it go over budget. The completion guarantor will carefully review the proposed budget, the track record of both Producer and Director and the commercial value of the film. If the completion guarantor is confident the film can be brought in on budget, a completion bond will be issued but not until all other financing has been raised and placed in escrow for the production.

## NO PRESALES FOR MOST LOW BUDGET FILMS

Unfortunately, it is very difficult for first time filmmakers to finance their movie based on presales. Presales are usually reserved for films with budgets over 5M (and definitely over 10M), as you must be able to attract a cast of a certain cachet. Presales also require the backing of bond companies since without completion guarantees, no bank will be willing to monetize them. Lastly, with no significant track record, the first time Producer will find it hard to persuade any distributor to pre-buy their work.

Still, if this is your first time producing but all other elements are in place as part of an attractive package (acclaimed writer, reputable director, several big name actors, etc.), a distributor may be persuaded to take a risk.

## PARTNERING WITH PRODUCTION COMPANIES

In the absence of a track record, a first or second time producer, writer, or director should consider partnering with a more experienced producer or production company in order to leverage their reputation and get your project made. If you work with a seasoned professional, you can learn the business and make new valuable contacts so that you're in a position to produce your next film on your own.

---

# CROWDFUNDING

Crowdfunding means using the Internet as a way of raising money for your film. You are reaching out to a "crowd" of people to "fund" your film with donations. Anyone can donate from as little as a few dollars to as much as a few thousand. Instead of paying back loans or a share in the profits, you offer rewards. It's a donation. Not an investment interest. Why is this important? As of 2012, the law prohibits crowdfunding platforms from offering equity investments in the projects they're supporting based on the SEC securities registration requirements. (See JOBS Act)

## REASONS TO USE CROWDFUNDING

Depending on the budget, there are several ways for filmmakers to take advantage of this resource. If you're working on a low budget film, you can actually raise a significant portion of the entire production costs. In the case of high budget films, you can use crowdfunding to pay just for legal expenses such as drafting a PPM, forming an LLC and putting together your Operating Agreement. Some producers even use this money to pay a casting director to get name actors attached to their film in order to increase their chances of getting foreign presales. At the recent 2012 Sundance

Film Festival, 15 films used crowdfunding as part of their budget strategy for an average amount of $35,000 per film.

## HOW DOES CROWDFUNDING WORK

How does this particular form of donating work? It's actually pretty simple. All you have to do is visit one of the websites that specialize in crowdfunding such as Kickstarter or Indiegogo. After registration, you can put up a page featuring your trailer, a film synopsis, your sales pitch, bios, awards as well as a link to your film's own website.

Your next step is to set a goal for your fund-raising campaign. You determine the amount of money you're seeking to raise and the number of days for your campaign (usually 30–40).

## DIFFERENCE BETWEEN KICKSTARTER AND INDIGOGO

Kickstarter charges a 5% fee on all funds raised during an "all-or-nothing" campaign, but, if the funding goal is not reached, no fees are charged and the funds are returned to the donors.

IndieGoGo allows two options: Fixed Funding and Flexible Funding. Fixed Funding applies the "all-or-nothing" model to your campaign so if you don't meet your goal, you aren't charged any fees and the funds are sent back to the donors. In addition, it also allows Flexible Funding where a 4% fee on all funds raised during a campaign is charged, but if the goal is not met, a 9% fee applies.

There are a few other minor differences between the two sites which you will need to research before deciding which one's best for you.

## TYPES OF FILMS FOR CROWDFUNDING

Crowdfunding works best with cause-related films because there's a built-in audience who's already mobilized. Let's say your film deals with autistic children or spirituality. There are countless organizations with extensive e-mail lists and other data banks at your disposal. You can also use social media and blogs to instantly reach your target demographic.

What if you have a narrative feature instead of an issue driven documentary? Does crowdfunding still work for you? The answer is yes, crowdfunding can work for any type of film but the success of the campaign will be based on your ability to *build an audience* while you're still in the financing stage.

## BUILDING AN AUDIENCE

The good news is that you're not dealing with the SEC or foreign distributors or worrying about monetizing your incentives. In the case of crowdfunding, your financing source is your audience! So it's vital to know how to reach your potential viewers and build an audience.

**1. Build a strong team** — You cannot do this alone. You have to surround yourself with people willing to put in the necessary time and effort. It takes a variety of different skill sets to create a buzz and build the traction needed to reach your audience. You need people who can manage the website, reach out to organizations or expand the mailing list.

**2. Create a Good Marketing Strategy** — You need to be continually driving people to your project page. You must decide ahead of time how you'll be able to achieve this. Who's updating the site? Who's shooting and uploading new videos on a regular basis? Who's expanding email lists and introducing new incentives? Create a campaign with various phases. You may start with the web; then seek out larger donors to become Producers; and, finally, create various pledge parties for larger donors to meet the talent.

**3. Create a Good Website** — Make it vibrant and exciting with plenty of interactive features and great videos. Post a trailer of yourself pitching the film. It makes a huge difference. People want to invest in you personally just as much as the project itself.

**4. Create a Great Trailer** — It doesn't have to be costly, look studio made or even be well edited. But it has to have heart. A documentary needs to touch people on a personal level. A narrative feature, to capture the imagination.

**5. Give Away Incentives** — You get to decide the type of rewards you'd like to offer. Anything from a simple "Thank You" letter to awarding a Producer credit on the film. Here's a list of the most common donations:

## A DONATION FOR A SPECIFIC
## DOLLAR AMOUNT WILL GET YOU A:

$1  subscription to an e-newsletter with inside news about the film.

$5  "thank you" email.

$10  free download of a song in the film.

*At each higher level, you get everything previously mentioned plus . . .*

$25  CD of the film soundtrack album.

$50  poster and script signed by the stars.

$75  film t-shirt.

$100  chance to be an extra in the film*

$250  DVD of the film signed by the stars.

$300  video chat on Skype with the stars.

$500  your name in the end credits under "Thank You".

$1,000  invitation to the set, dinner with the stars and an opportunity to attend the Wrap Party*

$2,500  invitation to the red carpet Opening Night and After Party*

$5,000  Associate Producer Credit and a bona-fide film Producer credit on IMDB.

> **\*Legal Secret\*** To avoid any potential legal disputes, make sure you include on all invites the words "Travel is at your own expense."

> **\*Legal Secret\*** You can give away anything you want. From a stay at your bed and breakfast to mileage points or even freshly baked chocolate chip cookies, your incentives do not have to be directly related to your project.

**6. Create Partnerships** — Reach out to anyone who can help grow your campaign. Seek out individuals, groups or organizations with common interests. Extend your incentives to them so that they blast their membership on behalf of your campaign. Give out free tickets to the screening in exchange for sending out your announcement. As a result of your hard work, you are building both potential partnerships and an audience for your film.

**7. Leverage your social networks** — Use Facebook, Twitter and blogs to post updates several times a week. Make a concentrated effort to build up your Facebook and Twitter pages daily. Use bloggers to get the word out. Ask them to attach a link to your trailer and website on their blog. Bloggers are your best friends.

**8. Be Consistent** — Don't let up the pressure until you reach the "tipping point" for someone to make a donation.

**9. Matching funds** — If you can demonstrate to your private investors that your film already enjoys a strong following, you may be able to convince them to match your crowdfunding donations and so create for yourself a chance to raise additional equity.

**10. Provide detailed plan for donation** — Most people are liable to make larger donations, if they understand exactly how their donations will be used so it's important to be able to provide them with a detailed explanation.

## COSTS OF CROWDFUNDING

You must factor all crowdfunding costs in your total film budget and map out a detailed campaign plan to help you doing so. It should include the site fee (Kickstarter charges 5% if you meet your goal, IndieGoGo charges 4% if you meet your goal and 9% if you don't meet your goal) as well as the Amazon expense (which handles all transactions for these sites and charges a payment processing fee of 3%). Do not forget to include the cost of creating, acquiring, and shipping the rewards. If you use a fiscal sponsor that allows donations to be tax-deductible, there will be an additional fee of 5–7%; IndieGoGo, however, waives its fee if you use one of its partner fiscal sponsors. In the end, the total costs of your campaign could possibly be upward of 25% of the money raised. Make sure you spend the crowdfunding money in the same year that you received it or else the IRS may tax it as your personal income.

## CROWDFUNDING USED FOR DISTRIBUTION

Filmmakers should design their crowdfunding campaigns to drive their distribution in the future. While the short-term goal is to raise money, the ultimate goal is to get distribution. A successful crowdfunding campaign will help you make a trailer, create partnerships, generate press awareness, create a web presence and build a core audience. You can also use the crowdfunding results to show potential distributors that there is already an audience for your film. Last but not least, the increased awareness will drive up all your ancillary revenues including VOD, DVD and internet and television sales.

## EQUITY FINANCING VS CROWDFUNDING

Equity financing means raising funds by selling an investment interest in your film. When you approach a potential investor, you're essentially asking them to take a risk. If the film isn't profitable, they will lose their initial contribution. Otherwise, the investor shares a percentage of all profits.

Under current legislature, you are not considered to be selling an investment interest when using crowdfunding but simply soliciting *donations*. Why is this so important? If you are selling an equity interest in a film (i.e. using investors), the federal government requires you to register the deal with the Securities and Exchange Commission (SEC) unless you can find a suitable exemption. Invariably, all independent filmmakers avoid registration with the SEC since the process is prohibitively expensive and extremely time consuming. As of 2012, no such viable exemption exists which would allow you to avoid SEC registration when using crowdfunding for equity investments.

## NEW LAW—JOBS ACT

In April 2012, President Obama signed the Jumpstart Our Business Startups (JOBS) Act, a new law that relaxes regulations to raise equity for startup companies in an effort to assist entrepreneurs.

When the new law becomes effective in 2013, it will allow filmmakers to: 1) raise up to one million dollars in equity investments without many of the prior securities restraints; 2) potentially use 2000 accredited investors and 500 non-accredited investors without forced registration; and 3) use internet crowdfunding to freely and publicly solicit, market and advertise to investors.

Prior to the new law, filmmakers were not allowed to publicly solicit investors for equity financing, *unless* 1) the filmmaker registered the offering with the SEC (an expensive and time consuming process); or 2) used an exemption to avoid registration.

Essentially, the JOBS Act creates a new Crowdfunding exemption from SEC registration. This Crowdfunding exemption includes the following requirements: 1) no more than $1,000,000 can be raised by crowdfunding in any 12 month period; 2) limits investors with a net worth under $100,000 to invest the greater of a) $2000; or b) 5% of their annual income or net worth (whichever is greater); or investors with a net worth over $100,000 can invest 10% of their annual income or net worth (no more than $100,000); and 3) the filmmaker must conduct the funding through a registered broker or "funding portal."

The JOBS Act requires filmmakers to file lengthy disclosure documents that include 1) information about your production company; 2) names of directors, officers and shareholders; 3) a business plan; 4) prior tax returns; 5) the target amount; 6) the share price; 7) details about the allocution of revenue; 8) the capital structure, and 9) risks involved, to name but a few.

Filmmakers raising $100,000 or less must simply disclose the most recent year's income tax returns (if any) and financial statements certified as being true and complete by an executive officer of the company. Filmmakers raising over $100,000 to $500,000 must have all financial statements reviewed by a certified public accountant. Finally, filmmakers raising over $500,000 must provide comprehensive audited financial statements.

The Act is not finalized. As of April 5, 2012, the SEC has 270 days to add more regulations.

# CHAPTER 4

## NEGOTIATING PRODUCTION AGREEMENTS

Congratulations! You've already secured the rights, created a business entity and raised financing for your film. You're well on your way to turning your dreams into reality. The next step is to successfully negotiate your production agreements. Film production agreements are generally divided into two main categories: "above-the-line" and "below-the-line," the former including producers, directors, actors and writers.

All seasoned actors, directors and writers invariably belong to their respective labor unions, which were formed to protect them from unfair wages and poor working conditions. The Screen Actors Guild-American Federation of Television and Radio Artists (SAG-AFTRA) is the labor union representing over 150,000 film and television principal and background performers. Directors belong to the Directors Guild of America (DGA) while writers are part of the Writers Guild of America (WGA). Each organization has its own set of rules and if a producer chooses to work with one of its members, the producer must sign a signatory agreement to follow its established rules and regulations with respect to minimum compensation, hours worked, pension and health contributions, work conditions, etc.

The following negotiation strategies and legal secrets will take the guesswork out of key production agreements. The agreements are not union agreements. However, the agreements closely parallel many of the union's major deal points including each member's services, compensation, term and credit so that you can focus on successfully putting together the strongest deal possible.

---

# PRODUCER AGREEMENTS

A clear understanding of the producer agreement is essential not only for producers themselves but also for directors, writers and anyone else interested in the film business. On your long and adventurous "journey to Ithaca," the producer is the key decision maker. He acts as the principal boat builder and his broad range of responsibilities is often divided between two distinct roles: the creative producer and the "line" producer. The obligations of the creative producer include securing the script, raising financing, hiring the director and casting. The "line" producer's duties, on the other hand, consist of bringing the film within budget, staying on schedule and ensuring timely delivery of the final product. Since the production company that hires the independent producer does not necessarily represent him, it is in his best interest to have a firm grasp of the major deal points when negotiating his contract. In the following example, the producer is responsible for both developing the deal and managing film production.

## PRODUCER AGREEMENT

**THIS AGREEMENT**, effective as of _____, 20__ is made by and between _____ ("Company") whose address is _____ and _____ ("Producer"), whose address is_____ with respect to Producer's services on the motion picture currently entitled "_____" (the "Picture").

> **Introductory paragraph.** This paragraph should not be taken lightly because it contains the effective date which may subsequently control some of the terms of the contract. Since the parties rarely sign the agreement on the same day, it is important to establish the date right at the top rather than running the risk of having two different dates next to the signatory lines at the end of the contract.
>
> It also introduces both parties — the production company and the producer — to the contract and states the film title.

1. **SERVICES**: Producer shall render all services customarily rendered by producers in the motion picture industry during all phases of production (i.e. development, pre-production, principal photography and post production) of the Picture. Services are to be rendered in accordance with the schedule mutually agreed upon between the parties, and will be at Company's direction in all respects.

> **Services.** These are the services a producer is expected to provide. This clause, however, is left intentionally vague with no particular list of obligations specified. What does "customarily rendered" mean exactly? The production company's attorney prefers to keep it ambiguous so that any service can be implied without having to name it individually.
>
> The services "customarily rendered" by the producer usually include the following:
>
> During the development stage: attending story meetings, supervising screenwriters, participating in casting, suggesting potential directors, preparing a budget, scouting locations, etc.
>
> During pre-production and principal photography, the producer's in charge, among other duties, of preparing the budget, securing locations, handling below-the-line agreements and supervising the accounting staff. He ensures the overall smooth operation of the production by ironing out any tensions that may arise between the cast, production company and/or director.

> During post-production, the producer assists in the editing process and supervises looping, dubbing and any potential reshoots.

2. **TERM:** Producer's Services have previously commenced and shall continue until the full and satisfactory completion of all Services to be rendered by Producer hereunder or the earlier termination of this Agreement. Producer's Services shall be exclusive during pre-production and principal photography. Producer's Services shall be non-exclusive, but first priority for all other times during the Term.

> **Term.** It deals with the length of time the producer will work on the film. In this instance, it is clearly specified from the very first sentence that the producer will remain employed until the full completion of all the services that were supposed to be rendered by him.

> **\*Legal Secret\*** Note that the word Services is capitalized. A capitalized word in the middle of a sentence always signifies that particular word has been previously defined so you have to make sure you look for the definition and are clear about the terms of the contract.
>
> Another important point is the difference between "exclusive" versus "non-exclusive." Producers generally don't want to be tied down to one project and would rather work on a non-exclusive basis — which means they can be involved with several films at the same time.
>
> The production company, on the other hand, prefers to employ the Producer on an exclusive basis so that he has to dedicate his entire time on their own project.

> **Pre-Production and Principal Photography.** (third line on Paragraph 2) During pre-production and principal photography,

the production company requires the producer to be available to render his services on an exclusive basis. This effectively means he cannot work on other projects during this time period.

**Development and Post-Production.** During "all other times", however, which means development and post-production, a compromise is usually reached between producer and production company. As stated in the last sentence of Paragraph 2, the producer can work on the production company's project on a "non-exclusive, first priority basis." This frees up the producer to work on other projects but as the term "first priority" implies, only if they don't interfere with this film.

3. **PRODUCTION OBLIGATIONS**: Producer shall put forth best efforts to cause the Picture to be (a) produced in accordance with the budget and production schedule approved by Company; (b) delivered within the time period specified in the post-production schedule approved by the Company, time being of the essence, subject to reasonable extensions for force-majeure events and (c) there will be no change without Company's prior consent, other than such minor changes in the approved screenplay required by the exigencies of production, but which will not alter the theme(s), story line or structure of the Picture or the characterizations contained therein.

**Production Obligations.** After having established what type of services a producer must provide, the way he's expected to deliver them becomes important.

These obligations are standard production guidelines. The first clause of Paragraph 3 deals with the budget and the production schedule by requiring the producer to follow costs closely and be able to anticipate any problems. Paragraph 3(b) expects the film to be delivered on time and 3(c) that the producer conforms to the approved screenplay.

> Regarding 3(b), the producer's attorney must always add a "force majeure" clause to the production obligations. It gives the producer more time to avoid breaching his contract due to circumstances beyond his control. Force Majeure means "superior force" in French and covers any unexpected event which may interfere with production including acts of God such as hurricanes, earthquakes, floods and fires; union strikes or even war. In reality, none of these eventualities are sadly as far-fetched as they may sound.

4. **COMPENSATION**: Provided Producer fully performs all services and obligations hereunder and are not otherwise in material breach of this Agreement, as full consideration of Producer's services hereunder, Company shall pay to Producer and Producer hereby accepts as complete consideration the following compensation:

   a. **Development Fee**. _____ Dollars ($_____), payable one-half upon Producer's commencement of services and one-half on Company's election to proceed to production or abandon the project.

   b. **Production Fee.** A total production fee of Three Hundred Thousand Dollars ($300,000.00). Such Production Fee shall be payable as follows:

      i. Twenty percent (20%) thereof in consecutive equal weekly installments over the schedule period of pre-production of the Picture, which shall begin on the date the Picture's website is launched.

      ii. Sixty percent (60%) thereof in consecutive equal weekly installments over the scheduled period of principal photography of the Picture.

iii. Ten percent (10%) thereof upon delivery of the rough cut of the Picture.

iv. Ten percent (10%) thereof upon completion and delivery to Company of the final cut of the Picture.

c. **Contingent Compensation.** Producer shall receive five percent (5%) of the Producer's share of net profits (i.e., 50% of 100% of the net profits), which shall be non-reducible. Producer's definition of net profits shall be no less favorable than Company's definition.

---

**Compensation.** It deals with the producer's remuneration by the production company. In the absence of any labor unions for producers, the production companies are not bound by any guild minimums.

The producer's fee is influenced by several factors including the following: the producer's quote, the box office performance of the producer's last film, any nominations or awards, the budget of the current film, the heat surrounding the producer and the nature of the services provided by the producer

A producer's compensation can be structured in many different ways. In this example, the contract contains a development fee, a production fee along with profit participation.

---

**Development Fee.** When the producer is part of developing the deal (i.e. finding the script, supervising writers, attaching actors or the director, etc.), he may be able to negotiate a development fee as an advance against his producing fee. Depending on the project, development fees range from $5,000 to $50,000. Look at 4(a): half of the development fee is usually paid upon commencement of services and half upon either the company's commencement or abandonment of the actual production.

---

**\*Legal Secret\*** Not all producers receive a development fee. Attorneys negotiate hard on behalf of their clients because they're aware most development projects end up not getting produced and this kind of fee may be the only money their client will ever see. Most of the time, all other fees are payable upon the film's completion.

**Production Fee.** It's usually a flat amount for the entire picture with payments spread over pre-production, production and post-production. Depending on the budget, a new producer's fees can range between $20,000 and $200,000 while established producers are able to command over $1,000,000 per film.

Payment Schedule: The production company typically imposes a payment schedule for the producer's production fee and it's commonly referred to as a 20/60/10/10 payment plan. Take a look at 4 (a) i–iv to understand what that means: 20% during preproduction, 60% during principal photography, 10% upon delivery of the rough cut and 10% upon delivery of the final cut.

**Contingent Compensation.** All producers generally negotiate for profit participation, meaning if the film is successful, they get a share of the profits. It's called contingent compensation precisely because it's dependent upon the film making profits.

**\*Legal Secret\*** The operative words in the producer's contingent compensation are whether it's payable from the "net profits" or the "gross profits."

Simply put, the gross profits are comprised of money from theatrical sales, VOD, home video, television, foreign sales, merchandising, music, etc.

Net profits is the amount of money left over after all allowable deductions which may include distribution fees and expenses, the negative cost of the picture, interest and financing charges,

> overhead charges, gross and deferred participations. Needless to say, net profits usually amount to nothing.
>
> Established producers are usually successful in negotiating some form of adjusted gross profits with the production company. New producers, on the other hand, have to settle with a percentage of net profits.

**5. CREDIT**: Provided Producer fully performs all services and obligations hereunder and the Picture is completed with Producer, and provided that Producer is not terminated for material breach or default of this Agreement, Producer shall receive the following credit:

"Produced by _____"

a. Producer's credit will be in the main titles, whether at the beginning or end of the Picture.

b. Producer's credit will be on a single card and shall appear in all positive prints of the Picture in the billing block of and all paid advertisements (subject to standard exclusions), with size, color, boldness and duration comparable to that of Company's credit.

c. All other aspects of credit and all other credits shall be at the sole discretion of Company.

> **Credit**. Producers should pay close attention to all aspects concerning their own credit. In reference to screen credit, they must negotiate for: 1) the location of their credit in the main title; 2) a separate card (as opposed to a shared card) where no other onscreen credits can appear at the same time as the producer credit; 3) how the size of their credit (i.e. width, boldness, etc.)

compares to the titles of other above-the-line talent (i.e. director or actors), and, finally, 4) once the screen credits have been determined, the producers should request to have their credit included in all of the film's paid advertising materials.

## 6. APPROVALS AND CONTROLS:

a. Company and Producer shall share equally approvals and controls of all kinds and nature, with respect to the Picture, including, but not limited to, all decisions involving artistic taste and judgment. Notwithstanding, once the parties mutually agree on the Approved Budget, Producer shall have all necessary controls to ensure the Picture is produced on-budget. Producer shall manage the day-to-day finances of the Picture, including signing checks and hiring below the line crew, upon reasonable consultation with Company. Any decision by Producer that may increase the Approved Budget shall require the prior written approval of Company, and similarly, any decision by Company that increases the Approved Budget will require a commitment by Company of the necessary additional investment. The parties acknowledge that the script of the Picture is completed and hereby approved.

b. If after good faith discussions, the parties come to an impasse on a decision related to the Picture, Company shall have the right to make the final decision.

**Approvals and Controls**. Otherwise known as who calls the shots.

Established producers seek approval rights over all creative elements of the picture such as principal cast, key crew members, the final draft of the screenplay, music, locations,

> shooting schedule, even the budget and the marketing campaign.
>
> Inexperienced producers may be able, at least, to obtain consultation rights when dealing with the aforementioned creative elements.
>
> Even when a producer is granted approval rights, however, the Company will reserve the right to make the final decision in the event of a disagreement with the producer.

7. **TERMINATION**: Company shall have the right to terminate this Agreement, effective immediately, if one of the following occurs:

   a. Producer fails to fully perform Producer's Services or fails to cure a material breach of this Agreement within forty-eight (48) hours of receipt of written notice of same;

   b. Death, illness, disability or incapacity of a principal cast member, director, producer or director of photography of the Picture, which exceeds ten (10) days; or

   c. A Force Majeure event which exceeds six (6) weeks, reduced to three (3) weeks during principal photography, in which event, Producer shall also have the right to terminate this Agreement.

> **Termination**. It basically allows the production company to fire the producer.
>
> As stated in subsection (a), the company can terminate the producer if he "fails to fully perform Producers Services". Notice that the word Services is capitalized so it refers to an item previously defined. In the very first paragraph of the contract, the language was kept intentionally vague so that it covers everything.

**\*Legal Secret\*** It's important for Producers to negotiate for a "right to cure" so if they subsequently manage to fix the problem, there will be no grounds for termination.

Most producer agreements allow the company to terminate the producer in the event of his death, disability, or incapacity. In the subsection (b) of this example, notice the right to terminate it is not limited the Producer.

Finally, in subsection (c), there is again mention of "force majeure" ("superior force" in French) covering any unexpected event that may interfere with production including acts of God such as hurricanes, earthquakes, floods and fires; union strikes or even war.

8.  **ARBITRATION**: All disputes under this Agreement shall be settled pursuant to binding arbitration under the rules of the Independent Film and Television Alliance ("IFTA") before a single arbitrator. The prevailing party will be entitled to reasonable attorney fees and costs.

**Arbitration**. This is especially important, if you are an independent Producer. You should always add an arbitration clause to the contract. Instead of dragging a dispute through court that could take years to adjudicate and incur astronomical legal fees, it's in both parties best interest to have agreed in advance to arbitration. If you're unable to resolve a dispute between you, this is the fastest and cheapest way to have it settled. I strongly recommend using IFTA since all of their arbitrators are attorneys who specialize in independent film.

9.  **TRANSPORTATION/ACCOMODATIONS**: Company shall provide all necessary transportation and accommodations for Producer in connection with the Picture as pre-approved and reasonably required throughout pre-production, production and post-production.

> **Transportation/Accommodations**. If a producer has to travel more than 50 miles from his principal place of residence to render services, he should request first class travel and accommodations as well as a minimum per diem. The extent of these provisions depends on the producer's stature and the film's budget.

## 10. MISCELLANEOUS:

a. <u>Festivals and Premieres</u>. Company shall invite Producer and a guest to all premieres and film festivals in connection with the Picture. Producer and his guest's transportation and accommodations for such premieres and festivals shall be on a most favored nations basis with any other individual working on the Picture.

b. <u>DVD</u>. Company shall provide Producer with one (1) copy of the Picture in DVD form when it becomes commercially available. Use of said copy by Producer shall be limited to private home use only.

> **Miscellaneous**. Producers must request an invite (for at least two people) to all premieres and festivals. If any of them are located more than 50 miles from his principal residence, he should ask the company for travel, accommodation, per diem and ground transportation. Low budget film companies will limit this type of perk to a domestic single premiere although it's advisable to have the producer attend all film related events for publicity purposes. Finally, every producer should request a copy of the DVD version of the picture when the DVD becomes commercially available.

**IN WITNESS WHEREOF** the parties hereto have caused this Agreement to be duly executed and delivered as of the day and year first above written.


PRODUCTION COMPANY          PRODUCER



_____          _____

By:                              By:
Its:     Managing Member

---

## NEGOTIATING THE DIRECTOR AGREEMENT

If the producer is the principal ship-owner, the director would be the vessel's indisputable master and commander. His creative input is necessary in every phase of the filmmaking journey such as developing the script (pre-production), coordinating cast and crew (principal photography) or supervising the film editing (post-production). Inevitably, the director agreement reflects his role at the helm and although similar to other above-the-line contracts, it also makes specific provisions for creative control, a director's cut, post production and even subsequent production services. In the following agreement, some of the major deal points will be highlighted so you are empowered to negotiate your rightful place behind the steering wheel with as much confidence as possible.

# DIRECTOR AGREEMENT

**Re:** **(Name of Production Company) -w- (Name of Director)/ "(Name of Picture")**

Dear **(Name of Director)**:

THIS AGREEMENT, effective as of _____, 20____ will confirm the agreement ("Agreement") between _____ **(Name of Director)** ("Director"), located at _____, and _____**(Name of production company)** ("Producer"), located at _____ regarding Director's directing services on the feature-length motion picture currently entitled "_____" (the "Picture") as follows:

---

**Introductory paragraph.** This paragraph should not be taken lightly because it contains the effective date which may subsequently control some of the terms of the contract. Since the parties rarely sign the agreement on the same day, it is important to establish the date right at the top rather than running the risk of having two different dates next to the signatory lines at the end of the contract.

The introductory paragraph also introduces both parties — the production company and the producer — to the contract and states the film title.

---

## 1. SERVICES:

**a. Development Services**. Director shall render such development services in connection with the Picture as are customarily rendered by directors of first-class, theatrical motion picture projects and as required by Producer, including without limitation the supervision of the development of the screenplay for the Picture. Such development services shall be rendered by Director on a non-exclusive, first priority basis.

**b. Production Services**. Director shall render all such services in connection with preproduction, principal photography and post production of the Picture as are required by the Producer and customarily rendered by directors of first-class feature length motion pictures and director shall comply with all reasonable directions and requests of Producer in connection therewith, whether or not the same involve matters of artistic taste or judgment. Director shall render such production services on an exclusive basis.

---

**Services.** The opening clause of the contract deals with the services that must be provided by the director and, in this example, are divided into two parts: development and production.

---

**Development.** Look at the first sentence under 1(a) "Development Services." The exact nature of these services is left intentionally vague with no particular list of obligations specified. What does "customarily rendered" mean? The producer's attorney prefers to keep it ambiguous so that any service can be implied without having to name it individually.

---

The services "customarily rendered" by the director at the development stage usually include attending development meetings, collaborating with writers on the screenplay, participating in casting or scouting locations.

**Exclusivity.** Look at the last sentence under 1(a) "Development Services." During development, directors generally don't want to be tied down to a single project and would rather be involved in several at the same time on a "non-exclusive" basis. Producers, on the other hand, prefer to have a Director work on an exclusive basis so that he has to dedicate his entire time on their own film.

Here, the respective attorneys negotiate a compromise. During development, the director is engaged on "non-exclusive" terms which frees him up to work in other projects but still on a "first priority basis" which implies that he may do so, only if they don't interfere with this film.

**Production:** Once again, the first sentence under 1(a) "Production Services" is left intentionally vague with no list of services specified. What does "customarily rendered" mean? It's all encompassing.

The services "customarily rendered" by the director during the subsequent stages of the film process usually include:

**Preproduction:** collaborate with writers on script development, assist the casting director with hiring the appropriate actors, conduct rehearsals, create a practical shooting schedule and plan the "look" of the film with the help of production designers and the director of photography.

**Principal photography:** address lighting issues, deal with everything related to camerawork, deal with blocking (how scenes are staged), confer with the sound crew, direct and advise the actors and decide what will be printed.

**Post production:** work with editor on editing, work with digital artists on visual effects and work with composer on music and scoring.

> **Exclusivity**. Look at the last sentence under 1(b): "Director shall render such production services on an exclusive basis." During production (i.e. preproduction, principal photography and post production), most producers require that the director is available to render his services on an exclusive basis which means he's not allowed to work on other projects during this time period.

**2. COMPENSATION:** Producer shall pay to Director the following compensation:

**a. Fixed Compensation:**

    **i. Development Fee.** _____ Dollars ($\_\_\_\_\_), payable one-half on fulfillment of the Conditions Precedent and one-half on Producer's election to proceed to production or abandon.

    **ii. Production Fee.** _____ Dollars ($\_\_\_\_\_), (less the Development Fee) payable 20% over pre-production, 60% over the period of principal photography, 10% upon completion of dubbing and scoring, and 10% upon complete delivery of the Picture in accordance with Producer's standard delivery specifications.

    **iii. Pay or Play.** Producer shall not be obligated to use Director's services on the Picture, nor shall Producer be obligated to produce, distribute, advertise, exploit or otherwise make use of the Picture; provided, however, that the full amount of the Fixed Compensation hereinabove specified shall be paid to Director should Producer elect not to utilize Director's services.

**b. Contingent Compensation.** Director shall be paid an amount equal to 5% of 100% of Producer's Net Proceeds, if any, derived from the Picture.

**c. Box Office Bonuses.** Director shall be entitled to receive the following box office bonuses within ninety (90) days following the initial publication of such worldwide theatrical box office gross receipts as reported in *Daily Variety* ("Sales"):

i. Fifty thousand dollars ($50,000) when the Picture reaches Sales in an amount of Fifty million dollars ($50,000,000);

ii. Fifty thousand dollars ($50,000) when the Picture reaches Sales in an amount of One Hundred million dollars ($100,000,000); and

iii. Fifty thousand dollars ($50,000) when the Picture reaches Sales in an amount of One Hundred Fifty million dollars ($150,000,000).

---

**Compensation.** It deals with the director's remuneration by the producer which is fully negotiable in the case of a non-DGA contract as in this example.

Several factors generally determine the director's compensation, some of which may be: the director's quote; the box office performance of the director's last film; any nominations or awards; budget of the present film; and, the heat surrounding the director.

A director's compensation can be structured in many ways. In this example, the contract contains a development fee, a production fee, profit participation and bonuses.

---

**Development Fee.** As stated in 2(a)(i), the development fee is a flat payment and, for independent films, usually can range from a few hundred dollars to $10,000.

**\*Legal Secret\*** Not all directors get a development fee. Attorneys negotiate hard on behalf of their clients because they're aware this kind of fee may be the only money a director will ever see since most development projects end up not getting produced and all other fees are payable only upon the film's completion.

**Production Fee.** It's usually a flat fee although producers impose a type of payment schedule commonly referred to as a 20/60/10/10 payment plan. Take a look at 2 (a) ii to understand where the name comes from: 20% during preproduction, 60% during principal photography, 10% upon completion of dubbing and scoring and 10% upon delivery of the Picture. For a film to be considered "delivered", it must first meet the Producer's standard delivery specifications. "Delivery" does not simply mean handing over the film.

**"Pay or Play"** Now, look at 2(a) (iii): The "pay or play" clause ensures that even if a producer ends up not using his director's services, the director is still entitled to his full compensation. So if the producer decides to have him replaced or simply halts production, the director is still paid.

The term "pay or play" signifies that the director either gets to "play" by directing the film (and gets paid) *or* that there is no play but he still gets to receive his "pay" (and gets sent home).

For example, let's say you are a director with a "pay or play" directing deal for $500,000 and a week into production the producer loses confidence in you. What happens in this scenario? The producer is still obligated to pay you $500,000 just to send you home. Of course, if the producer loves you, he's more than happy to let you play, direct the film and reward you for your effort accordingly.

**\*Legal Secret\*** Many directors have a false sense of confidence when it comes to being "pay or play." A shrewd entertainment attorney, however, is aware that it all hinges upon what point in time the director becomes "pay or play." When does it exactly attach? When I'm representing the director, for example, I negotiate that pay or play attaches as soon as the director signs the contract (DAY 1). When I'm representing the producer, on the other hand, I make sure it attaches as late as possible and that could be mean either once financing is secured, or the first day of shooting or a whole month into it (DAY 30).

**"Pay and play"** is a very prestigious clause to have in your contract and only a select few directors are able to command it. The producer must both pay the director AND play him (use his services). It essentially means that the director cannot be fired.

Once again, whether a director becomes "pay OR play" or "pay AND play" depends on their bargaining power. And, in the first instance, the real clout lies with when the provision attaches.

**Contingent Compensation.** All directors generally negotiate for profit participation which means, if the film is successful, they get a share of the profits. It's called contingent compensation precisely because it's dependent upon the film making a profit.

The tricky part of the negotiation is whether the director's contingent compensation is payable from the net or gross profits.

Simply put, the "gross profits" are comprised of money from theatrical sales, home video, television, foreign sales, merchandising, music, etc.

"Net profits" is the amount of money left over after all allowable deductions which may include distribution fees and expenses, the negative cost of the picture, interest and financing charges, overhead charges, gross and deferred participations. Needless to say, net profits usually amount to nothing.

Most first-time directors only get 5% of net proceeds.

**Box Office Bonus.** This form on payment is based on box office performance as determined by *Daily Variety* or some other reputable trade magazine. Directors should always ask to have it included in their contract, as it's more objective than net profits. If the picture succeeds in generating a particular level of theatrical box office gross receipts, the director is entitled to additional compensation: if box office is 50M = $50,000, if box office is 100M = $50,000 and if box office is 150M = $50,000. This payment is cumulative.

3. **CREDIT**: Provided the Picture is released, and provided Director shall have rendered and completed Director's services in principal photography of the Picture, Producer agrees to accord Director credit, in accordance with the requirements contained in the DGA Basic Agreement, substantially as follows:

"Directed by _____"

Director shall not receive a possessory credit unless Producer, in its sole discretion, deems such credit to be appropriate.

**Credit.** All aspects of credit must be negotiated when a film is not subject to the DGA. Look at the first sentence of our example, however. Most non-DGA films tend to follow DGA requirements regardless.

The most important requirements contained in the DGA Basic Agreement deal with 1) placement 2) size and 3) advertising.

In reference to placement, the DGA requires that the "directed by" credit must be the final onscreen credit appearing in the main titles and, in their absence, it must be the first credit of the end titles.

In reference to size, the DGA requires that the director's credit cannot be smaller than 50 percent of the film's title.

In reference to advertising, the DGA provides minimum requirements for the director's credit to be included in certain paid advertising including: Print ads, Billboards, Radio ads, One sheets. Exclusions are awards, nominations and congratulatory ads.

**Possessory Credit.** Besides the "directed by", many experienced directors may ask for an extra "film by" credit. As this addition isn't governed by the DGA, however, all aspects of it must be negotiated. Highly prestigious, it's one of the very few credits to appear on screen even before the film title.

## 4.  APPROVALS AND CONTROLS:

a.  Producer shall solely have all approvals and controls of all kinds and nature, with respect to the Picture, including, but not limited to, all decisions involving artistic taste and judgment. Notwithstanding, Producer shall meaningfully consult with Director on all material creative elements of the Picture, including the hiring of talent and key crewmembers.

b.  **Director's Cut**. Director shall be entitled to make one (1) cut of the Picture (the "Director's Cut") as required pursuant to the DGA Basic Agreement. Director's right to prepare the Director's Cut shall be conditioned upon (a) Director not being in material default of the Agreement; and (b) Director preparing and delivering the Director's Cut in conformance with the requirements set forth in this Paragraph.

i. The choice of editing location shall be at Producer's sole discretion.

ii. Director shall deliver to Producer the Director's Cut of the Picture no later than eight (8) weeks after the completion of principal photography. The Picture, as delivered, shall (i) strictly adhere to the final approved shooting script (subject to such minor changes required by the exigencies of production and as approved by Producer), (ii) be no less than ninety (90) minutes and no more than one hundred twenty (120) minutes in length (including main and end titles), (iii) be in color in a standard thirty-five millimeter (35mm) format, and (iv) qualify with the Motion Picture Association of America ("MPAA") for a rating no more restrictive than "R", unless Producer agrees in writing to a more restrictive rating.

iii. Nothing in the foregoing or elsewhere in this Agreement shall in any way limit Producer's absolute and final cutting authority with respect to the Picture or to otherwise modify, edit, add to and delete from the Picture at any time as Producer may determine in its sole discretion.

---

**Approvals and Controls.** As a general rule, the producer retains complete and unconditional control over the entire picture including the right to cut, add to, or modify it any way he sees fit. In short, he makes all final decisions as stated in 4(a).

Most experienced directors, however, will fight hard for the contractual right of approval over all major creative elements such as principal cast, key crew members, final draft of the screenplay, music, locations and schedules in order to safeguard their vision.

Even if they're successful in their negotiations, the producer will always reserve the right to have final say, as he's the one who controls the money and would like to keep it that way.

**Director's Cut.** Under DGA regulations, the producer must accord the director the opportunity to complete a director's cut of the film. High profile directors such as Kathryn Bigelow, Oliver Stone, George Lucas or Steven Spielberg are able to command "final cut" of the theatrical release version of the film. All other directors should negotiate the right to create a "director's cut" upon the film's release on home video and DVD.

5. **SUBSEQUENT PRODUCTIONS:** Provided Director is not in material breach hereof, the Picture's negative cost does not exceed 110% of the Approved Budget, the Picture is delivered in accordance with the mutually approved delivery schedule, Director is then actively engaged as a director in the motion picture industry and Director is available to render directing services as, when and where reasonably required by Producer, then, if Producer desires to produce a theatrical sequel, prequel, remake (collectively, "Subsequent Production") within five years after the initial domestic release of the Picture, Producer will negotiate in good faith with Director concerning Director's services with respect to the first Subsequent Production on terms to be negotiated in good faith and in accordance with industry standards for comparable engagements.

**Subsequent Productions.** If there is a subsequent production (i.e. prequel, sequel, remake, etc.), the producer will negotiate with the director for his services all over again. Most directors welcome the opportunity to be involved once more although the inclusion of this clause in their contract by no means constitutes a commitment on the producer's part but more of an assurance that the original director will be the first to be asked.

> **\*Legal Secret\*** Producers will sometimes require that a new director commits to directing a second picture at a pre-negotiated price, hoping to lock him in at a price potentially lower than his future market value.

**6. TERMINATION**: Producer shall have the right to terminate this Agreement, effective immediately, if one of the following occurs:

a. Director fails to fully perform Director's Services or fails to cure a material breach of this Agreement within forty-eight (48) hours of receipt of written notice of same;

b. Death, illness, disability or incapacity of a principal cast member, Director, producer or director of photography of the Picture, which exceeds ten (10) days; or,

c. A Force Majeure event which exceeds six (6) weeks, reduced to three (3) weeks during principal photography, in which event, Director shall also have the right to terminate this Agreement.

> **Termination**. It basically allows the producer to fire the director.
> As stated in section 6(a), the producer can terminate the agreement if the director "fails to fully perform Directors Services". Notice that the word Services is capitalized so it refers to an item previously defined. In the very first paragraph of the contract, the language was kept intentionally vague so that it covers everything.
>
> **\*Legal Secret\*** Directors must negotiate for a "right to cure" so if they manage to subsequently solve the problem, there will be no grounds for termination.

> Most agreements allow the producer to terminate the director in the event of his death, disability, or incapacity. In the subsection (b) of this example, however, this agreement is not limited to the Director's death or disability.
>
> Finally, in subsection (c), the director's attorney must always add a "force majeure" clause. It gives the director more time to avoid breaching his contract due to circumstances beyond his control. Force Majeure means "superior force" in French and covers any unexpected event which may interfere with production including acts of God such as hurricanes, earthquakes, floods and fires; union strikes or even war. In reality, none of these eventualities are sadly as far-fetched as they may sound.

7.  **TRANSPORTATION/ACCOMODATIONS**: Producer shall provide all necessary transportation and accommodations for Director in connection with the Picture as needed throughout pre-production, production and post-production. Specifically, Producer shall provide Director with:

   a.  One first-class round-trip air transportation (if available and if used), from [Los Angeles] to location.

   b.  Ground transportation to and from the airports and set.

   c.  DGA scale per diem.

   d.  Living accommodations (i.e., one first-class hotel room or equivalent accommodations).

> **Transportation/Accommodations.** Directors working on non-DGA productions must negotiate all aspects of transportation and accommodations.
>
> Under DGA regulations, if a director has to travel more than 50 miles from his principle place of residence to render services,

> he's entitled to first class travel and accommodations as well as
> a minimum per diem.

8. **FESTIVALS/PREMIERES:** Producer shall provide Director and a guest to all premieres and film festivals in connection with the Picture. Director and his guest's transportation and accommodations for such premieres and festivals shall be on a most favored nations basis with any individual Producer. Additionally, Director shall be reimbursed for all reasonable documented expenses upon receipt of such documentation.

> **Festivals/Premieres.** Directors should negotiate for an invite
> (for at least two people) to all premieres and festivals as well as
> travel, accommodation, per diem and ground transportation. Low
> budget film producers may limit these perks to a single domestic
> premiere even though it's advisable to have the Director attend
> all film related events for publicity purposes.

9. **DVD/SOUNDTRACK:** Director shall receive, free of charge, when commercially available, one (1) copy of the soundtrack (if any) and one (1) DVD copy of the Picture. Such DVD and soundtrack shall be used for personal purposes only; Director shall not have the right or authority to use the print for any other purpose including without limitation exhibit, distribute or make copies of the DVD or Soundtrack.

> **DVD/Soundtrack.** Directors should always request a DVD copy
> of the film and its soundtrack when they become commercially
> available.

**10. ARBITRATION**: All disputes under this Agreement shall be settled pursuant to binding arbitration under the rules of the Independent Film and Television Alliance ("IFTA") in Los Angeles, California before a single arbitrator. The prevailing party will be entitled to reasonable attorney fees and costs.

> **Arbitration.** This is especially important to the Director. Always add an arbitration clause to the contract. Instead of dragging a dispute through court which could take years to adjudicate and incur astronomical legal fees, it's in both parties best interest to have agreed in advance to arbitration. If you're unable to resolve the matter, this is the fastest and cheapest way to have it settled. I strongly recommend using IFTA because all of their arbitrators are attorneys who specialize in independent films.

Very truly yours,

_____

**ACCEPTED AND AGREED:**

_____

**("Director")**

# NEGOTIATING THE ACTOR AGREEMENTS

During your long and adventurous "journey to Ithaca", actors act as guiding lights. In today's largely "name" driven market, they are the indisputable stars of the show. Securing a recognizable face is critical for attaining financing and producing a feature film. As a result, performers can be very demanding during negotiations because they're the only creative element who appears on screen as well as in all advertising and promotion. It is essential to have a clear grasp of the nuances of the actor agreement since they are usually the most challenging deals to navigate.

The Screen Actors Guild-American Federation of Television and Radio Artists (SAG-AFTRA) is the labor union representing professional film and television actors. Its basic agreement establishes the minimum compensation for its members, the maximum hours they're allowed to perform and general working conditions. The following simplified agreement parallels a standard SAG-AFTRA actor agreement and outlines some of the major deal points you need to consider during negotiations so that the stars align in your favor.

## ACTOR AGREEMENT

**THIS AGREEMENT**, effective as of _____, 2009, is made by and between _____ ("Producer") and _____ ("Artist"), with respect to Artist's portrayal of the role "_____" in the production of the motion picture currently entitled "_____" (the "Picture").

**Introductory paragraph.** This paragraph should not be taken lightly because it contains the effective date that may subsequently control some of the terms of the contract. Since the parties rarely sign the agreement on the same day, it is important to establish the date right at the top rather than running the risk of having two different dates next to the signatory lines at the end of the contract.

It also introduces both parties — the production company referred to as the "Producer" and the Actor referred to as the "Artist" — to the contract, states the role the Actor will portray as well as the film title.

1. **SERVICES**: Artist shall render all such services as are required by the Producer and **customarily rendered** by actors in first-class feature-length theatrical motion pictures in the motion picture and television industry, at such times and places required by the Producer, and to comply with all reasonable directions, requests, rules and regulations of the Producer in connection therewith, whether the same involve matters of artistic taste or judgment.

**Services.** These are the services an actor is expected to provide. This clause, however, is left intentionally vague with no particular list of obligations specified. What does "customarily rendered" mean in the first sentence? The production company's attorney prefers to keep it ambiguous so that any service may be implied without having to name it individually.

The services "customarily rendered" by the actor usually include:

**During Pre-production:** pre-production meetings, readings, rehearsals, costume fittings, make-up and hairdressing tests, photo and recording tests, publicity stills, etc.

**During Production:** principal photography, stunts (if any), trick shots, publicity stills and "Making of" interviews, etc.

> **During Post-production:** looping, dubbing, added scenes and retakes, soundtrack recording, additional publicity and promotional interviews, etc.

2. **START DATE**: Artist shall render services hereunder exclusively to the Producer in connection with the principal photography of the Picture commencing on a date to be designated by the Producer ("Start Date") and continuing for ten (10) consecutive weeks thereafter ("Guaranteed Period") or until completion of principal photography of the Picture, whichever is later. **The Start Date is presently contemplated by the Producer to be on or about** _____.
In addition, Artist shall render services in connection with rehearsals and pre-production of the Picture commencing on a date to be designated by the Producer and continuing until the Start Date. After the completion of principal photography, Artist shall be available for customary post-production services, subject to his/her then existing prior professional commitments.

> **Start Date.** It deals with when the actor is expected to start rendering their services. Other than compensation, an actor's availability is the most important area of negotiation.
>
> Coordinating the start date is a delicate balancing act as the performer wants it to be specific whereas the producer prefers to keep it flexible in case the production is delayed. The producer also needs to have the date determined well in advance so there's enough time for pre-production and financing.
>
> **\*Legal Secret\*** The producer should avoid using the words "on or about (the start date)" because, according to SAG, "on or about" strictly refers to "one day before or after" the date specified. Instead, he should always negotiate for "approximately two weeks plus or minus (the start date)".

3. **COMPENSATION**: Upon condition that Artist fully performs all Services required hereunder and Artist is not in default hereunder, the Producer agrees to pay to the Artist, as full and complete consideration for such services and for all rights transferred by Artist to the Producer hereunder, the following:

a. Guaranteed Compensation: The sum of _____ Dollars ($_____) ("Guaranteed Compensation") accruing in ten (10) equal weekly installments commencing on the Start Date.

b. Deferment: Provided that the Artist shall appear recognizably in the Picture as released in the role in which Artist is engaged hereunder, a contingent deferment ("Deferment") in the amount of _____ Dollars ($_____) payable, if at all, out of the first sums which would otherwise constitute "net proceeds" of the Picture.

c. Contingent Compensation: Upon condition that the Artist appears recognizably in the Picture as released in the role in which the Artist is engaged hereunder, the Artist shall be entitled to receive an amount equal to _____ percent of one hundred percent (_____% of 100%) of the net proceeds, if any, of the Picture.

---

**Compensation.** It deals with the actor's remuneration.

This is usually the first deal point to be negotiated between the producer's attorney and the actor's agent with three different basic types available: 1) guaranteed, 2) deferred and 3) contingent compensation.

An actor's compensation can be influenced by many factors including:

---

**SAG Minimums.** For SAG actors, it's pretty straightforward. The established minimum is provided based on the film's budget and the nature of the services requested. Keep in mind, it is only the minimum. For that reason, many actors negotiate "scale plus ten" which means an additional ten percent to cover their agent's commission.

**The Actor's Quote.** As with other talent, the producer will take into consideration what an actor was able to command for similar work in the past. Available quotes are usually used as floors for further negotiations.

**The Heat Surrounding the Actor.** If the actor wins a prestigious award such as an Academy Award, Golden Globe or Emmy, their subsequent fees will reflect this honor even if they were paid scale for their most recent acting assignment. For example, Natalie Portman's fees undoubtedly skyrocketed after her critically acclaimed and award winning performance in *Black Swan*.

**The Budget Size.** The film budget often plays a key role in determining the actor's compensation. For example, if the entire production costs $10M, it would be impossible for a producer to pay Will Smith his current quote of at least $20 million as an upfront fee. Instead, a backend deal must be negotiated.

**The Talent Involved in the Film.** Many stars will forgo their sizeable upfront salaries for the opportunity to work with a talented producer or director. For example, Leonardo DiCaprio took a 90% cut on his fee to be able to work with Clint Eastwood on *J. Edgar*. An actor can then negotiate a more significant backend participation.

**The Role.** The size of the role and the length of the term also determine the actor's compensation. A lead role with a full schedule commands a higher fee than a cameo appearance.

**Guaranteed Compensation**

It's the amount of money an actor is guaranteed to receive no matter what. Acting fees are generally paid in equal weekly installments over the scheduled period of principal photography.

For example, if the actor is promised $100,000 for ten weeks of work, he will end up getting $10,000 per week.

**\*Legal Secret\*** In fact, this may prove trickier than it may initially appear depending on what's exactly considered to be the scheduled period. If you pay an actor $100,000 for ten weeks of principal photography, does that include rehearsals? What about pre-production? Or even post-production? What if you go over principal photography? Is there an overtime provision? Is it the weekly amount divided by five? Or is it divided by six? It makes a big difference.

Obviously, the producer would like to negotiate one all-inclusive price and the actor would like to be paid extra for each additional service rendered. It all comes down to each party's individual negotiating power.

### Deferred Compensation

This type of payment is delayed until some later point in time.

When an actor accepts less money up front than his usual quote in order to help the movie get made, he will frequently negotiate a "deferred compensation."

In this increasingly popular practice, the actor receives the first sums of the net proceeds once they come into the producer's possession. It should be noted that the deferment is always a specific dollar amount rather than a percentage.

### Contingent Compensation

This type of payment is called contingent because it depends on the film turning a profit.

**\*Legal Secret\*** You must pay close attention to whether the actor's contingent compensation is payable from the net profits, adjusted gross profits or first dollar gross.

**Gross Participation** — Simply put, gross profits are comprised of money from theatrical sales, VOD, home video, television, foreign sales, merchandising, music, etc. Producers will carefully grant true gross participation to talent since that would entitle them to a percentage of all revenues received by the producer with no deductions of any kind.

Only stars in the caliber of Will Smith and Julia Roberts are able to secure an amount approaching true first dollar gross participation which guarantees them a share in the producer's revenues with limited "off the top" deductions such as taxes, trade dues and residuals.

**Adjusted Gross Receipts** — The main difference between gross and adjusted gross participation is that, in addition to "off the top" deductions, the distribution fee (between 10–40%) gets also subtracted before the actor gets a percentage.

**Net Participation** — Net profits are the amount of money left over after all allowable deductions which include distribution fees and expenses, the negative cost of the picture, interest, financing and overhead charges, gross and deferred participations. Needless to say, net profits usually amount to nothing.

As with most deal points, the greater the actor's leverage, the more favorable his participation.

4. **CREDIT**: Provided Artist is not in material breach of this Agreement, Artist shall receive a credit, in substantially the following form:

   a. [CREDIT — Artist's name]

   b. [Artist's credit will be in the main titles of the Picture on a [single/shared] card] OR [Artist's credit will be in the end titles of the Picture] and shall appear in all positive prints of the Picture and all paid advertisements, subject to standard exclusions.

c. Paid Advertisements: Artist's credit shall be included in any paid advertisements for the film, other than an award, nomination or congratulatory-type advertising crediting only another individual.

d. All other aspects of credit and all other credits shall be at the sole discretion of Producer.

---

**Credit.** Unlike the WGA or DGA, the SAG Agreement does not closely regulate credits so actors have to carefully negotiate a variety of issues including:

**Placement.** Most actors request that their on-screen credit appears on a separate card in the main titles. Producers generally refuse such privileges to talent with smaller roles who only receive credit on a shared card along with other actors of comparable stature. In the case of minor participation, the credit will be simply placed in the end titles.

**Position.** There is usually an initial jockeying for the first and second positions. If there are several stars in the film and all desirable placements have already been taken, many agents demand that their client receives the "and [actor's name] as [character name]" OR "with [actor's name]" card at the end of the credit sequence. A way of simplifying arrangements is by alphabetical order or order of appearance.

**Size.** Stars may receive a credit equal in size to 100% of the film title. Most actors, however, request their credit be no less the size of any other player in the film, including its height, width, boldness and on-screen duration. Producers often have no problem granting this as long as the credit's still smaller than that of the lead actor.

**Paid Advertisement.** It designates all ads taken out and paid for by the film producer or distributor for promotional and publicity purposes, including movie posters ("one sheets"), billboards, magazine and newspaper ads or radio and television spots. Only stars receive this credit.

## 5. TRANSPORTATION AND EXPENSES:

a. When Artist's services are required by Producer to be rendered hereunder at a place more than fifty (50) miles outside of Artist's then principal place of residence, Producer shall furnish Artist with or reimburse Artist for

1) one (1) round trip transportation from said residence to any said location (transportation shall be provided on a commercial airline first-class where Artist is required to fly at the request of Producer);

2) reasonable accommodations, and

3) a per diem allowance for meals of no less than $____ Artist agrees to furnish Producer with itemized accountings for all such expenditures which shall comply with the Internal Revenue Service's regulations, including substantiating vouchers, invoices, and receipts relating to such expenses.

**Transportation and Expenses.** It specifies the type of transportation and amount of spending money actors are entitled.

The SAG Agreement requires that its members travel first class and, if necessary, by air and they are driven to and from all airports, hotels as well as the set. Although it doesn't provide for first class accommodation, it must be reasonable. Finally, if meals aren't included, a per diem has to be paid.

**6. DRESSING FACILITIES**: At all times when Artist is required to render services hereunder, the Producer shall provide the Artist with separate dressing facilities, if available.

> **Dressing Facilities.** Studios can afford and often offer their stars lavish dressing facilities. On location, the typical trailer may have a bed, bathroom with shower along with a separate living area while being equipped with satellite TV, stereos, telephones and other amenities.
>
> Independent producers who generally can't provide comparable luxuries should negotiate instead a clause promising the actor the "best available" dressing facility within the parameters of the budget. Also, add a clause that "no other star will receive a more favorable dressing facility."

**7. STILLS/LIKENESS APPROVAL:** Artist shall approve (not to be unreasonably withheld or delayed) not less than fifty percent (50%) of all submitted publicity stills for the Picture in which Artist appears alone and seventy five percent (75%) for group stills, with such stills to be provided in groups. Artist will be required to provide Artist's disapproval within three (3) business days after delivery to Artist or Artist's representative (unless Artist is advised that marketing exigencies require a sooner response), or approval will be deemed given.

> **Stills/Likeness Approval.** When an actor attains a certain level of recognition, the producer will accord them still photos and drawn likeness approval rights.
>
> Here, the actor will be able to approve 50% of all pictures of themselves intended as promotional or publicity material as well as 75% of group shots.
>
> In reference to drawn likeness approval rights, a producer may either grant one, two or three "passes" which means the actor has up to three chances to make changes to the submitted likeness.

8. **PUBLICITY AND PROMOTION SERVICES:** Artist will be available for interviews and other customary events to help promote the Picture. If Artist is requested to travel for such purpose, Artist will then be advanced or reimbursed for first class travel and expenses for Artist.

> **Publicity and Promotion.** Besides the acting services, a performer's guaranteed compensation is generally deemed to include all of the required publicity and promotional duties such as attending press junkets, giving interviews, posing for still photos, making promotional films and trailers or any behind-the-scenes footage.
>
> First-class travel and expenses are generally provided, if an actor's presence is required outside their principal place of residence.
>
> If further publicity and promotion services are expected after production is complete, the actor usually negotiates that it is subject to the actor's then-pre-existing contractual commitments or professional availability.

9. **FESTIVALS/PREMIERES:** Producer shall provide Artist and a guest to all premieres and film festivals in connection with the Picture. Producer shall provide Artist and his guest's transportation and accommodations for such premieres and festivals Additionally, Actor shall be reimbursed for all reasonable documented expenses upon receipt of such documentation. Notwithstanding the foregoing, all screenings, premieres, festival and related expenses shall be subject to distributor's approval.

> **Festivals/Premieres.** Actors should secure an invite (for at least two people) to all celebrity screenings, premieres and festivals whereas stars can further request travel, accommodation, per diem and ground transportation. For producers, it's important

> to make these types of commitment subject to the distributor's approval since they are expensive and the producer may not be able to meet them. It's advisable, however, to have all stars attend all premieres and film festivals for publicity and promotion purposes.

10. **ARBITRATION:** If not subject to the SAG arbitration provisions, disputes under this Agreement shall be settled pursuant to binding arbitration under the rules of the Independent Film and Television Alliance ("IFTA"). The prevailing party will be entitled to reasonable attorney fees and costs.

> **Arbitration.** This is especially important for independent producers. Always add an arbitration clause to the contract. Instead of dragging a dispute through court which could take years to adjudicate and incur astronomical legal fees, it's in both parties best interest to have agreed in advance to arbitration. If you're unable to resolve the matter, this is the fastest and cheapest way to have it settled. I strongly recommend using IFTA because all of their arbitrators are attorneys who specialize in independent films.

IN WITNESS WHEREOF the parties hereto have caused this Agreement to be duly executed and delivered as of the day and year first above written.

PRODUCER                          ARTIST


_____          _____

By:                               By:

## "BELOW THE LINE" AGREEMENTS

What about the people toiling away below deck so to speak? Usually referred to as Crew Deal Memo, the "below the line" agreement covers a wide variety of crewmembers such as grips, drivers, lighting technicians, make-up artists, art directors and costume designers. With the exception of a few deals (i.e. the cinematographer, music supervisor, composer and costume designers), "below the line" deals are pretty straightforward. Although each crewmember offers a different type of service, many of the contracts for "below the line" personnel address the same basic issues: services, compensation, credit, meals, travel, lodging and per diems. In the following section, some of the major deal points found in below the line agreements will be highlighted.

### Services

"Below the line" personnel are often hired under a short form employment agreement or even a simple deal memo with the provision addressing their services drafted in very broad and vague terms. In fact, all that's often indicated is that workers must provide customary services consistent with industry standards. The length of service, however, is very clear and producers specify how each employee is hired: "at will" which means the crew member can be replaced for any reason; "week to week" which secures pay for the entire week even if employment is terminated before that; or for the "run of the show" which guarantees remuneration for the duration of the production.

### Compensation

Most "below the line" personnel are represented by one of two labor unions: IATSE (International Alliance of Theatrical and Stage Employees) or the Teamsters. When a producer hires a union member, he's obligated to sign a collective bargaining agreement which means the crewmembers will be employed at union-prescribed rates. In the case of a non-union film, however, the producer can get away with only paying a flat weekly rate with no need for additional overage fees if the shoot goes into overtime on certain days.

## Credit

"Below the line" credits generally appear during the end titles of a movie. Certain professions, however, (i.e. Production designer, Costume designer, Cinematographer, Casting Director, Editor and Composer) are considered higher-profile and so able to negotiate for their name to appear in the main film title. Subject to applicable collective bargaining agreements, Producers usually negotiate that any crewmember's screen credit is at his own discretion and contingent upon them performing all required services until the completion of the project.

## Meals/Travel/Lodging/ Per Diems

The production company provides meal breaks and/or food service at approximately six-hour intervals. Additional meals are sometimes included three hours after crew call and lunch. If the crew is on location, they are usually provided with travel expenses, lodging and per diem.

## Work for Hire

A smart producer will also include a "work for hire" clause in the "below the line" agreement. Many of the unique creations of various crew members (i.e. Set Designer, Costume Designer and the Cinematographer) can be potentially protected under a copyright in their own name. In order to avoid any future legal disputes dealing with rightful ownership, it should be specified in the contract that the producer will be the sole and exclusive owner of the employee's services.

## Conclusion

The line producer is usually responsible for negotiating all "below the line" employment agreements directly with the crewmembers being hired. You should discuss, however, any pertinent questions that might arise with an entertainment attorney.

# CHAPTER 5

## NEGOTIATING MUSIC AGREEMENTS

How about suitable dramatic background music while you're sailing out on the vast blue seas during your long journey? A little melody enhances everything and there are two main ways to obtain it for your movie. You can either hire a composer to create especially for you or you can just use pre-existing music not initially intended for film. In this section, the major issues surrounding the latter option will be examined so you can sway all the way to your final destination.

### PRE-EXISTING MUSIC

Pre-existing music, when not in the public domain, has two separate copyrights: 1) the copyright in the song (the written lyrics and music); and 2) the copyright in the sound recording (an artist's master of the song). For example, the song "(You Make Me Feel Like) A Natural Woman" was written by songwriter Carole King, but sung by performing artist Aretha Franklin on a sound recording. Therefore, if a producer wanted to use Aretha Franklin's recording of Carole King's song, he would have to negotiate with the copyright owners of both the song and the sound recording.

When a producer chooses a pre-existing piece of music, he doesn't buy the copyright itself but obtains a "license" from its legal owner(s) to use that particular song and/or sound recording. A license is written permission from the copyright owner to use the music in the film. As a result, the producer must obtain two such written permissions: a "synchronization license" for the song and a "master use license" for its sound recording of the song.

## Synchronization License

In order to use a song, the producer must obtain a synchronization ("synch") license from its rightful owner(s) which would allow him to reproduce it on the soundtrack of the movie in synchronization with the filmed images. This would mean the publisher, if the song-writer has already sold or assigned their copyright in that piece of music. Or, in the absence of such a deal, songwriters may license their own work and the producer will have to negotiate directly with them.

A wide range of variables help determine the synch licensing fee. For instance, its intended usage plays an important part in the negotiations. Is it background music, actually performed in the movie or used as the film title? The length and popularity of the song are also deciding factors. An unknown song in a small budget independent film cannot command the same fees as a popular one in a studio blockbuster.

### Master Use License

When a producer uses a pre-existing sound recording, he must first obtain a master use license which allows him use of the master of the song in the film. This can usually be done through the artist's record company or, in the absence of such a deal, directly through the artist provided they still own the master recordings.

The licensing fee can be influenced by several factors including the stature of the artist, the popularity of the song, its length and intended use in the film. It can range anywhere from several hundred dollars for an unknown artist to several thousands of dollars for the work of someone famous.

Worldwide rights must also be secured by the producer for the full term of the copyright and in all media, including television rights, VOD, home video, interactive and multimedia.

Licensing pre-existing music for a soundtrack can prove very complex because producers have to obtain the correct licenses according to the particular requirements of their movie. Failure to properly clear music in advance can prove disastrous because its rightful owner(s) can subsequently have a court issue an injunction to prohibit distribution of the film or charge exorbitant fees for the privilege. At which point, the producer will find himself in a severely compromised negotiating position with his only choices either to pay the inflated price or remove the music from the film.

## SONGS CREATED FOR THE FILM

Many film producers would rather hire artists to write songs especially for their film rather than go through the trouble of "clearing" and obtaining licenses for pre-existing songs. If the chosen talent is already under contract with a record label or publisher, permission must be obtained to avoid any potential legal problems.

### Work-For-Hire

In a typical publishing deal, half of the income is paid to the artist (writer's share) and the other half to the publisher (publisher's share). It's in the producer's best interest, however, to employ any potential talent on a "work for hire" basis so that he's automatically considered the sole owner for copyright purposes. This is especially important for low-budget independent productions.

## COMPENSATION

In order to keep upfront fees to a minimum, film producers can share their publishing income with the writer/artist. Rather than pay huge fees on the front end, they can split their back-end publishing income 50/50 with the writer/artist. As owners of the publishing rights, producers will be then in a position to negotiate with the artist/writer to split the following main sources of publishing income: performance royalties, record royalties (mechanicals) and synchronization income.

## Public Performance Royalties

Every time a song is played in a public setting (movie theaters in foreign territories only, television, radio, etc.), it generates income for its rightful owner. Both writer/artists and publishers are represented by public performance societies (ASCAP, BMI and SESAC) who are responsible for licensing songs, collecting fees and paying out public performance royalties. When negotiating the deal, it should be emphasized that all such income is paid directly to the writer/artists by the public performance societies. Otherwise, they'd be dependent on the producer's accounting practices or have to wait for his quarterly statements.

## Movie Theatres

Due to U.S. anti-trust laws, no public performance income is generated from movie theatres in the country. That is not the case abroad, however, where a 2.5 to 5% of ticket price can be retained. Even for a limited theatrical release, publishing income can be as high as $150,000 since it's not tied to the film's actual profits but to the number of screenings.

## Television

Both within the U.S. and in foreign territories, public performance royalties are generated every time a film is shown on television (i.e. cable, pay, network and syndication). The public performance societies (ASCAP, BMI or SESAC) negotiate with television companies for blanket royalties for all songs. Based on cue sheets, TV companies pay out the corresponding royalties to the public performance companies so that they can forward them directly to their members avoiding any delays caused by the film producer's accounting practices.

## ADDITIONAL COMPENSATION

### Record Royalties (also known as Mechanicals)

Record royalties are generated through sales of the record. Profits are calculated by a percentage of the wholesale retail price in foreign territories and by a flat rate (currently 9.1 cents) per song within the U.S. For example, if the producer accords the writer/artist all of the publishing and there are ten songs on the soundtrack album then they will earn 91 cents per album sold (at full statutory rate). So, at 100,000 albums, the songwriter stands to make $91,000 in record sales.

### Synchronization Income

Synchronization income is generated every time a writer/artist's songs are used in another film, television program, commercial, songs video, etc. by way of a licensing fee (a "synch" license). When the film producer owns the synchronization rights, he's entitled to all revenue but it's possible for the songwriter to share in it as well according to the terms of the negotiation.

## OTHER MAJOR CONTRACT ISSUES

### Rights

The film producer should seek to obtain the broadest nature of rights from the writer/artist in order to have unlimited ownership of all aspects of the songs. If a writer/artist is employed on a "work for hire" basis then the producer automatically retains unlimited ownership of all aspects of the songs. In that case, he's entitled to freely use the material not only in the present film but also in any sequels, remakes, advertising, trailers, etc.

## Credit

The most common form of credit is "Song By (Writer's Name)" and it's usually buried somewhere in the film's closing credits. As a bargaining tool, however, a producer can grant the writer/artist responsible for the majority of the songs, a separate, single-frame card credit of "Songs By" during the same sequence. Or, if necessary, the producer can even make available a spot in the film's opening credits along the names of the stars, producers and director.

> **\*Legal Secrets\*** It's very common for the budget to have been exhausted by the time independent film producers reach post-production. In order to sweeten the deal for potential composers, producers must be willing to offer back-end royalties and non-financial terms. When used as bargaining tools, these sources can provide producers with the necessary leverage to obtain the desired songs for the film.

## NEGOTIATING THE MUSIC SCORE CREATED FOR FILMS

In order to enhance a film, producers frequently hire composers to create an underscore. Also referred to as the "score," it's the music heard underneath the dialogue, action, transitions, etc. A well-crafted score can greatly intensify the overall impact a movie has on its audience.

The composer's agreement contains various complex deal points so it's best for an experienced entertainment attorney to handle the negotiations. What follows is an overview of some of the key terms of the standard agreement between composer and producer (independent production company).

## COMPOSER AGREEMENT

**THIS AGREEMENT**, effective as of _____, 20__, is made by and between [YOUR NAME/COMPANY] ("Producer") whose address is [PHYSICAL ADDRESS] and [COMPOSER] ("Composer") whose address is [PHYSICAL ADDRESS].

> **Introductory paragraph.** This paragraph should not be taken lightly because it contains the effective date which may subsequently control some of the terms of the contract. Since the parties rarely sign the agreement on the same day, it is important to establish the date right at the top rather than running the risk of having two different dates next to the signatory lines at the end of the contract.
>
> It also introduces both parties — the Producer and the Composer — to the contract.

## 1. SERVICES:

**(a) Score.** Composer shall compose, record, produce, and deliver an original musical score in accordance with instructions from Company ("Score") for the Picture. Composer's services shall not include orchestration or conducting. The Score, the record mixes of the Score ("Score Masters"), and all results and proceeds of Composer's services hereunder are collectively referred to as the "Work".

**(b) Non-Score Musical Works.** If Company desires Composer to write and produce non-Score musical works, Company shall negotiate with Composer in good faith.

> **Services.** The film producer must define the scope of the composer's services. In a very close collaboration, the composer will be usually responsible for overseeing all aspects of creation of the underscore which include: composing the entire score of the film, orchestrating the music, conducting the orchestra, producing, recording and editing the arrangement, and delivering the final master recording according to schedule.

## 2. COMPENSATION:

**(a) Guaranteed Compensation.** Provided Composer is not in material breach of this Agreement, in consideration of Composer's services hereunder, Producer shall pay to Composer and Composer hereby accepts as complete consideration Two Thousand Five Hundred Dollars ($2,500), payable 50% on signing and 50% on delivery of final mix of music.

> **Guaranteed Compensation.** Composing fees vary widely depending on the stature of the composer, the film budget, the type of music required, the orchestra size and how the agreement is actually structured. There are two basic ways to put together such a contract. First, "the package deal" in which the composer is provided with a fund that includes his creative fee and, in return, assumes responsibility for the entire cost of the music production. The alternative is for the composer to receive a lesser creative fee solely for his composing and conducting services but without being liable for any additional expenses incurred.

**(b) Publishing Rights.** With respect to the exercise of publishing rights in the Work, Composer shall be entitled to fifty percent (50%) ownership of the "Publisher's share," for the Work, the other fifty percent (50%) of which shall belong to Producer.

Additionally, Producer and Publisher shall administer their respective shares, as in this case, fifty/fifty (50%/50%).

> **\*Legal Secret\*** In order to keep the guaranteed compensation to a minimum, independent film producers can negotiate to split their publishing income 50/50 with the composer. Instead of paying upfront fees, producers can pay with back-end publishing royalties.

(c) **Other Royalties**. If the master recordings of the Work are exploited in any manner other than in the soundtrack of the Film, such as, included in phonorecords or published as sheet music, Producer shall pay, or will cause the record company distributing the phonorecord to pay to the Composer, an appropriate royalty, which will be negotiated in good faith and based on industry standards.

> **\*Legal Secret\*** Producers should always consider splitting royalties from other sources of exploitation of the material as a strategy to lower the upfront guaranteed compensation of the composer.

3. **TERM**: The term hereof shall commence upon the date set forth above and shall continue until satisfactory completion of Composer's services, during which time Composer's services shall be non-exclusive first priority. The Work is to be delivered to Company no later than (**Date**).

> **Term.** The composer's services generally begin after principal photography is finished. Occasionally, however, his participation is also required during that period when he's asked to review the film along with its producer and director in order to determine the best placement for the music. The term is complete once the music has been "dubbed" into the final edited version. In an

independent film, the producer may negotiate for the composer to have the entire score written and recorded within three to five weeks. And if the picture is behind schedule or over budget, he will be forced to complete it in an even shorter amount of time.

## 4. COMPOSER ENGAGING OTHERS:

(a) To the extent that Composer engages the services of other individuals (e.g., lyricists, orchestrators, singers and musicians) in connection with creation of the Work in connection with the Picture, Composer represents and warrants that it will be solely responsible for obtaining grants of rights, releases and representations and warranties from those individuals as broad and inclusive as Composer's own, throughout the world, in perpetuity and in all media, in order to enable Producer to exploit the Work free and clear of any claims relating to (i) use of any material and/ or equipment utilized by Composer in connection with the Work (other than the material supplied by Producer) and (ii) the performances of any persons rendering services in connection with the Work (other than persons engaged by Producer). Such persons will be creating works made for hire for Producer. Composer agrees to indemnify Producer from any and all claims arising out of Composer's failure to obtain sufficient grants of rights, releases and representations and warranties under this paragraph. When requested, Composer will provide Producer with full and complete documentation of such grants, releases and representations and warranties. If union residuals are required to be paid, Composer will be responsible for such payments.

(b) Composer shall be solely responsible for and shall pay any and all costs and expenses incurred in the production and delivery of the Work including without limitation all costs and expenses relating to (i) all material and equipment utilized by Composer in connection with the Work (except for the material supplied by Producer) and (ii) all compensation, fees, royalties, and any other sums payable to all persons rendering services in connection with the Work (other than persons engaged by Producer); all tape and copywork; any fees payable to any guild or union as a result of the rehearsal, performance and recording of the Work and (iii) any other costs and expenses incurred in connection with the production of the Work. Producer shall not be required to make any payments of any nature for, or in connection with, the Work, except under union contracts growing out of the exploitation of the Picture.

> In the independent film world, most composer agreements are structured as "package deals." The composer is responsible for all expenses of putting together the score including musicians, recording, copying, orchestrators, instruments, cartage, payroll, etc. Many composers have their own studios and can minimize costs by using electronic synthesizers. Since all music is delivered fully recorded and for a fixed price, this approach favors the producer who knows in advance how much it's going to cost and that there will be no unexpected costs during postproduction.

5. **RIGHTS:** Composer hereby grants Producer rights to synchronize the Work in the Picture and thereafter to exploit the Picture, including the Work in all media whether now known or hereafter created in perpetuity throughout the universe, including in connection with advertising and promotion of the Picture. Composer further grants Producer the right to produce a soundtrack album based on the Picture, which may include the Work, in Producer's sole discretion.

## 6. WORK-FOR-HIRE:

(a) Composer hereby acknowledges that all of the results and proceeds of Composer's services produced for the Picture hereunder shall constitute a "work-for-hire" specially commissioned by Producer and Producer or Producer's assignee shall own all such results and proceeds. Producer may make such use of the Picture and distribution of the Picture as Producer, in its sole discretion, shall deem appropriate.

(b) If Composer's services are not recognized as a "work-for-hire," Composer hereby irrevocably grants, sells and assigns to Producer, its successors and assigns, all of Composer's rights, title and interest of any kind and nature, in and to the Picture, including, without limitation, all copyrights in connection therewith and all tangible and intangible properties with respect to the Picture, in perpetuity, whether in existence now or as may come into existence in the future.

(c) Composer waives the exercise of any "moral rights" and "droit moral" and any analogous rights however denominated now or hereafter recognized. All rights granted and agreed to be granted to Producer hereunder are irrevocable and shall vest and remain perpetually vested in Producer, its successors and assigns, whether this Agreement expires in normal course or is sooner terminated, and shall not be subject to rescission by Composer for any cause whatsoever.

> Since the producer hires the composer to remain under his direct supervision, most composer agreements are structured as "work for hire." In this type of contract, the producer is automatically

> granted for a flat fee total control and ownership of all music and recordings, and, consequently, all music publishing rights as well. The main sources of income for music publishers are public performance royalties, mechanicals (record royalties) and synchronization.

7. **CREDITS**: Provided that Composer's Work comprises more than fifty percent (50%) of the original musical underscore of the Picture as released, Composer shall receive credit on screen in the main titles of the Picture (whether at the beginning or end of the Picture) in substantially the following form:

**"Music by _____"**

> **Credit.** Established composers usually have their credit placed in the main titles and on a separate card which reads "Music by (composer's name)." If they are unknown, however, their name will most likely appear at the end of the film in the list of closing credits. As a bargaining tool, producers of low budget films can grant the composer a separate, single-frame card credit of "Music by" during the same sequence. Or even a spot in the opening credits where the stars, producers and director are listed.

8. **NAME AND LIKENESS**: Composer hereby grants to Producer the perpetual right to issue and authorize publicity concerning Composer, and to use Composer's name and likeness and biographical material in connection with the exhibition, advertising and exploitation of the Picture. Composer hereby covenants and agrees not to make any claim or bring any suit or action which will or might interfere with or derogate from Producer's rights under this Agreement.

9. **NO OBLIGATION TO PRODUCE**: Nothing contained in this Agreement shall be deemed to require Producer or its assignees to publish, record, reproduce or otherwise use the Work or any part thereof, whether in connection with the Picture or otherwise; and Composer hereby releases the Producer from any liability for any loss or damage Composer may suffer by reason of Producer's failure to utilize the Work. Payment of the Compensation at the time set forth shall fully discharge Producer of all its obligations hereunder. Producer may not use the Work except in connection with the Picture, the exploitation thereof (including a soundtrack of the Picture) and all advertising and promotion relating to the Picture.

10. **REPRESENTATIONS AND WARRANTIES**: Composer represents, warrants and agrees that it is free to enter into this Agreement and not subject to any conflicting obligations or any disability which will or might prevent Composer from, or interfere with, Composer's execution and performance of this Agreement; that it has not made and will not make any grant or assignment which will or might conflict with or impair the complete enjoyment of the rights granted to Producer hereunder; that, except for any material supplied to Composer by Producer, all material referred to in Paragraph 1 hereof will be wholly original with Composer or in the public domain throughout the world or based upon material furnished to Composer by Producer. Composer further warrants that said material will not infringe upon the copyright, literary or dramatic rights of any person.

11. **NO INJUNCTIVE RELIEF**: In the event of a failure or omission by Producer or any third party constituting a breach of Producer's obligations hereunder, the damage, if any, caused to Composer thereby shall be deemed not irreparable or sufficient

to entitle Composer to enjoin, restrain or seek to enjoin or restrain the development, production, distribution or exploitation of the Work, the Film, or any sequels, prequels, and/or Albums or other soundtrack recordings derived there from, or to seek any other equitable relief. Composer's rights and/or remedies in the event of a failure or omission constituting a breach by Producer of the provisions of this Agreement shall be limited to Composer's rights to seek damages in an action at law.

> **Injunction**. An injunction is a court order which could allow the composer to prevent the film from being distributed. It is imperative for producers to include this clause in order to limit the composer's rights to only being able to sue for money damages in case of dispute.

**12. ARBITRATION**. All disputes under this Agreement shall be settled pursuant to binding arbitration under the rules of the Independent Film and Television Alliance ("IFTA") before a single arbitrator in [STATE]. The prevailing party will be entitled to recover reasonable attorney fees and costs.

> **Arbitration.** This is especially important for independent producers. Always add an arbitration clause to the contract. Instead of dragging a dispute through court which could take years to adjudicate and incur astronomical legal fees, it's in both parties best interest to have agreed in advance to arbitration. If you're unable to resolve the matter, this is the fastest and cheapest way to have it settled. I strongly recommend using IFTA because all of their arbitrators are attorneys who specialize in independent films.

This Agreement constitutes the entire agreement between the parties hereto with respect to all of the matters herein and its execution has not been induced by, nor do any of the parties hereto rely upon or regard as material, any representations or writing whatsoever not incorporated herein and made a part hereof. No amendment or modification hereto shall be valid unless set forth in a writing signed by both parties.

**IN WITNESS WHEREOF** the parties hereto have caused this Agreement to be duly executed and delivered as of the day and year first above written.

PRODUCER                          COMPOSER


_____          _____
By: _____            SSN: _____
Its: _____

# CHAPTER 6

## DISTRIBUTING INDEPENDENT FILMS

### DISTRIBUTION OVERVIEW

Once you've succeeded in completing your filmic journey, wouldn't it be great if the whole world got to know about it? That's where the power of theatrical distribution comes into play and, like some mythical creature, it is certainly multi-headed.

First of all, of course, you want your movie to be seen in your home country. You might be in luck because with U.S. theatrical distribution this is one area where you can negotiate directly with the distributor without a need for a middleman. And this means more money in your pocket since you avoid having to split profits with a sales agent or producer representative.

If you're unable to obtain US distribution on your own, a producer rep can always help you. Film festivals can also become very useful vehicles for achieving your goal.

As far as foreign distribution is concerned, for aspiring filmmakers there's no way around working with an experienced sales agent. And film markets become your biggest allies in your quest for worldwide exposure.

Finally, there's always the DIY method of negotiating all your rights separately with various companies. With a little extra effort, self-distribution can become a reality. You've already come this far, nothing can stop you now.

## U.S. THEATRICAL DISTRIBUTION

In the independent film world, making a movie is not nearly as difficult as getting a good distribution deal. Securing a distribution deal can be more challenging than raising financing or even producing the entire film. Unfortunately, this isn't some kind of "if you build it, they will come" scenario. That only happened in the movie *Field of Dreams* and would be a huge mistake on the part of any aspiring filmmaker to believe that all it takes is a good film and distribution will be automatic. In reality, Distributors must feel confident enough they stand to make a solid return on their investment in order to justify the cost and time they will need to dedicate. And although not an absolute prerequisite, having a name director or star on board can improve the chances of securing distribution. Let's assume though the Gods have smiled upon you and there's a U.S. Distributor interested in your film. The following covers some of the major deal points of such an agreement.

**DISTRIBUTION AGREEMENT**
(All-Rights Deal)

THIS AGREEMENT made and entered into as of _____, 20__ is made by and between _____, ("Distributor") and _____ ("Producer"). In consideration of their respective covenants, warranties and representations, together with other good and valuable consideration, Distributor and Producer hereby agree as follow:

> **Introductory paragraph.** This paragraph should not be taken lightly because it contains the effective date which may subsequently control some of the terms of the contract. Since the parties rarely sign the agreement on the same day, it is important

to establish the date right at the top rather than running the risk of having two different dates next to the signatory lines at the end of the contract.

It also introduces both parties — the Distributor and the Producer — to the contract.

1. **PICTURE**: Producer will deliver to Distributor the documentation, advertising and physical materials (the "Materials") set forth in the Delivery Schedule (see Exhibit A), relating to the motion picture, currently entitled:

"_____" (the "Picture")

**Picture.** This clause may appear short and straightforward but it's really not. While it's obvious that it states the film title, it also happens to be laden with potential problems.

A film isn't considered properly "delivered" until all documentation, advertising and physical materials are in the distributor's possession. Ah, there's the potential problem!

For the delivery requirement to be fulfilled, every last one of the items listed in Exhibit A at the end of this chapter must be first furnished along with the film. And that's only a shortened version of material usually expected.

Many new filmmakers are under the false impression that simply sending the film to the distributor does the trick. It doesn't.

We will carefully review these documents when the time comes to examine the delivery clause. For now, all you need to remember is that if your film isn't properly "delivered," the distributor isn't required to do his part. And that means your film gets tied up indefinitely, no one will be able to see it and you won't get paid.

2. **RIGHTS GRANTED**: Producer hereby grants to Distributor the irrevocable, right, title and interest in and to the distribution

of the Picture, its sound, and music in the territory (as hereinafter defined) including without limitation, the sole, exclusive, and irrevocable right and privilege, under Producer's copyright and otherwise, to distribute, license and otherwise exploit the Picture, its image sound and music, for the term (as hereinafter defined) throughout the territory (as hereinafter defined) for Theatrical, Home Video/DVD, Television, Video On Demand(VOD), and Internet media.

Such rights do not include the rights to produce other motion Pictures, or sequels, or remakes of the Picture or any right to produce television series, mini series, or programs or other so-called ancillary rights (herein called "Reserved Rights").

---

**Rights Granted.** It refers to the rights a producer grants a distributor to exploit the film.

Pay close attention to the second to last line in the first paragraph. Here, the producer's granted the Distributor "theatrical, home video/DVD, television, Video on Demand and Internet media" rights. It is imperative to comprehend the value of your media rights.

Understandably, if a DVD or VOD distributor offers an advance to license a recently completed film, an overeager producer will probably jump at the opportunity without fully grasping the ramifications of his actions. In fact, it may be a grave mistake. You might as well forget about securing any theatrical distribution deal after that.

Domestic distributors know that many films actually lose money at the box office so they would never take on the financial risk of a theatrical release without having also secured the potentially more profitable ancillary rights (DVD, VOD, internet media and television).

---

3. **RESERVED RIGHTS**: All other rights not expressly written herein, including but not limited to, electronic publishing,

print publication, music publishing, live-television, radio and dramatic rights are reserved to the Producer.

> **Reserved Rights.** These are the rights filmmakers keep for themselves so that they can either self-distribute or engage the services of another distribution company.
>
> In this example, the Producer reserved all of the rights listed in paragraph 3.
>
> Needless to say, it's important to understand exactly what's been reserved so you can exploit these rights elsewhere.

4. **TERRITORY**: The territory (herein "Territory") for which rights are granted to Distributor consists of the United States, its territories, possessions & military bases, and English-speaking Canada.

> **Territory.** A territory is the country where a distributor has the right to exploit the film.
>
> **Worldwide** rights denote the right to distribute the film in any country in the world.
>
> Independent filmmakers often enter into more than one distribution deal in which case the rights are divided into two territories: domestic and foreign.
>
> **Domestic** usually means the U.S. and either English speaking or all of Canada. It may also include "U.S. territories, possessions and military bases."
>
> **Foreign** rights signify the rest of the world.
>
> **\*Legal Secret\*** Your best strategy is to give your foreign rights to a sales agent rather than the U.S. distributor. The vast majority of U.S. independent film distributors only serve domestic territories directly and employ sub-distributors for the rest of the world which means the producer ends up paying double fees.
>
> That's not to imply you should never allow a U.S. distributor

> to use sub-distributors. You need to know your numbers in
> advance and be able to determine who handles exactly what.
> If a filmmaker believes the use of a sub-distributor is beneficial
> in foreign territories, he should make sure to cap the distributor
> fees and go ahead and close the deal.

5.  **TERM**: The rights granted to Distributor under this Agreement
    will commence on the date of this Agreement and continue
    thereafter for two years (the "Initial Term"). If Distributor pays
    Producer $100,000 or more in the Initial Term, Distributor shall
    automatically have the right to extend the term for another two
    year term "a Subsequent Term"). During this Subsequent Term
    (and additional subsequent terms if extended), Distributor shall
    have the option of extending the term for additional two-year
    periods (up to a total term of no more than ten years) if the
    following thresholds are met:

    a)  Initial Term: If $100,000 has been paid to Producer, then
        Distributor may extend the term for another two years (the
        First Extended Term).

    b)  First Extended Term: If $200,000 cumulatively has been paid
        to Producer during the Initial and First Extended Term, then
        Distributor may extend the term another two years (Second
        Extended Term).

    c)  Second Extended Term: If $300,000 cumulatively has
        been paid to Producer during the Initial, First and Second
        Extended Term, then Distributor may extend the term for
        another two years (the Third Extended Term).

    d)  Third Extended Term: If $400,000 cumulatively has been
        paid to Producer during the Initial, and First through Third

Extended Term, then Distributor may extend the term for another two years (the Fourth Extended Term).

---

**Term.** It's the length of time the distributor has to distribute the film.

Distributors want a long term ranging from 10–15 years. They argue that in some cases they provide an advance and in all cases they spend a lot on marketing so are naturally after a longer term to be able to recoup their costs.

Such long terms, however, are not in your best interest. After the first few years, your film may be shelved and will continue to sit there gathering dust instead of being marketed until the term expires or you're forced to renegotiate the deal. The ideal initial length of time for filmmakers should be 2–4 years.

In that case, a subsequent extension can be provided but only if the distributor pays a certain amount of money. In clause 5 (a) of our example, an additional two years will be granted, if the producer earns at least $100,000 during the initial term. A series of similar rollovers may follow with the total number of years capped at ten.

---

6. **DELIVERY MATERIALS**: The Picture will be delivered as follows:

a) On or before _____ Producer will deliver to Distributor the materials specified in Exhibit A hereto, accompanied by a fully executed lab access letter (irrevocable for the term) for access to the Master materials. If any said materials are not acceptable to Distributor, Distributor will notify the Producer of any technical problems or defects within (10) business days and Producer will promptly replace the defective materials at Producers' sole expense. Distributor shall have no right to terminate this Agreement unless and until Producer has failed to cure any such defects within thirty (30) days after notice thereof from Distributor.

If no objection is made within ten business days of delivery of an item, the item will be deemed acceptable.

---

**Delivery Material.** As mentioned in the first clause, it refers to all documents and other material a filmmaker is obligated to provide in order to satisfy the delivery requirements for the film.

Exhibit A at the end of the contract contains a short delivery list which varies depending on the type of picture produced among other factors. A 35MM motion picture, for example, doesn't have the same requirements as a digital one.

**\*Legal Secret\*** Besides the specific content of each list, what can also prove tricky is that some distributors still like to play games when it comes to the delivery clause, using technicalities as an excuse to refuse an advance or delay payment to the producer. So before you sign on the dotted line, you must make absolutely certain: 1) you have all the items, or 2) you know you can get the items within a certain time period, or 3) you've succeeded in having a particular item removed, or 4) you've convinced the Distributor to help you pay for what you need. Some items on the list are negotiable.

---

7. **ADVANCE/GUARANTEE**: There shall be a non-refundable advance of $_____, payable on execution of this agreement.

---

**Advance/Guarantee.** An advance is the money you receive up front for licensing your film to a distributor.

Under current market conditions, distributors are willing to offer advances only if the movie benefits from highly marketable elements like name actors, producers and/or director, or acceptance by a major film festival.

Advances range from complete buyouts like *Little Miss Sunshine* or *Juno* by Fox Searchlight to a specific dollar amount (e.g. 200K–5M) against a certain percentage of net profits. In

---

> the last case, you would be getting an advance and once the distributor manages to recoup it along with all related expenses, they split the rest of the profits with you.
>
> Although distribution by a major independent distributor is an uphill battle for an independent film, you're far more likely to receive an advance if you succeed.

8. **ALLOCATION OF GROSS RECEIPTS**: As to proceeds derived from Distributor's exploitation of all rights outlined in Paragraph 2, division of the Gross receipts will be made, as follows:

   a) From the Distributors exploitation of Theatrical, Television, Home Video/DVD, Video on Demand, Internet and any other Granted Rights, Distributor shall deduct and retain twenty percent (20%) of Gross receipts.

   b) From the remaining revenues Distributor shall recoup all recoupable expenses related to the prints, marketing, advertising and sale of the Picture.

   c) The net proceeds shall be paid to Producer.

   d) Gross Receipts: As used herein, the term "Gross Receipts" shall mean all monies actually received by and credited to Distributor less any refunds, returns, taxes, collection costs and manufacturing or duplication costs.

   e) Deductions from Gross Receipts shall be taken in the following order:

      1) Distribution fee (20%)

2) Recoupment of any advance and any recoupable Delivery Expenses incurred by Distributor

3) Recoupment of any recoupable Print Expenses.

4) Recoupment of any recoupable Promotional Expenses incurred by Distributor.

5) Net Proceeds shall be paid to Producer.

---

**Allocation of Gross Receipts.** "Allocation of Gross Receipts" is just a fancy way of saying who gets what in the end.

In our example, subsection (a) makes it clear that the distributor earns 20% of all monies made across the board for his time and effort. In subsection (b), he also gets to recoup all expenses related to the distribution of the film. Finally, in subsection (c), the producer receives the remainder or what's called "Net Proceeds". Section (d) defines "Gross Receipts." While section (e) consists of a recap of the allocation of money.

---

9. **RECOUPABLE EXPENSES**: As used herein, the term expenses and/or recoupable expenses shall mean all of Distributor's actual expenses on behalf of the Picture limited as follows:

a) Promotional Expenses: These expenses include the cost of preparing posters, one-sheets, trailers and advertising. Distributor agrees to spend no less than $25,000 and no more than $40,000 on promotional expenses. These expenses are limited to direct out-of-pocket expenses actually spent on behalf of the Picture. At Producer's request, Distributor shall provide receipts for each and every expense or forgo recoupment. Recoupable promotional expenses do not include any of Distributor's general office, overhead, legal or staff expenses or any of the aforementioned Market Expenses. Distributor agrees to spend the minimum necessary to adequately promote the Picture, including preparation of a trailer, poster, one-sheet, videocassette and customary promotional material.

b) Delivery Expenses: Delivery Expenses are the direct out of pocket costs incurred by Distributor to manufacture any of the film or video deliverables (as listed on Exhibit A) which Producer did not supply. At Producer's request, Distributor shall provide receipts for each and every expense or forgo recoupment. Recoupable Delivery Expenses do not include any of Distributor's general office, overhead, legal or staff expenses or any of the aforementioned Promotional or Market Expenses.

---

**Recoupable Expenses.** It deals with the money a distributor has to spend in order to distribute your film.

This is where certain questionable accounting practices may come into play and two plus two doesn't always equal four.

You should always make sure your agreement clearly defines the type and amount of expenses the distributor is allowed to recoup.

**\*Legal Secret\*** Producers should negotiate to have a cap placed on all expenses as well as categorize them into two distinct groups: 1) promotional and 2) delivery expenses.

As defined in subsection (a), Promotional Expenses are incurred by preparing posters, one-sheets, trailers and advertising. The distributor should agree to a minimum amount of money to be spent (floor) as well as a maximum cap (ceiling).

In subsection (b), Delivery Expenses cover the distributor's costs to manufacture all of the film deliverables.

If you fail to keep proper track of distribution expenses, it's essentially money out of your own and your investors' pockets.

---

**10. ARBITRATION AND JURISDICTION:** Any controversy or claim arising out of or in relation to this Agreement or the validity, construction or performance of this Agreement, or the breach thereof, shall be resolved by arbitration in accordance with the rules and procedures of the Independent Film & Television Alliance (IFTA), said rules may be amended from time to time with rights of discovery if requested by the arbitrator. Such rules and procedures are incorporated and made a part of this Agreement by reference.

> **Arbitration.** This is especially important for independent producers. Always add an arbitration clause to the contract. Instead of dragging a dispute through court which could take years to litigate and incur astronomical legal fees, it's in both parties best interest to have agreed in advance to arbitration. If you're unable to resolve the matter, this is the fastest and cheapest way to have it settled. I strongly recommend using IFTA because all of their arbitrators are attorneys who specialize in independent films.

Paragraph headings in this Agreement are used for convenience only and will not be used to interpret or construe the provisions of this Agreement.

IN WITNESS WHEREOF, the parties have executed this agreement as of the date hereof.

_____     By:

_____     Its:

ACCEPTED AND AGREED:

_____

# EXHIBIT "A"
## DELIVERY REQUIREMENTS

Delivery of the Picture shall consist of Producer making delivery, at Producer's expense, to DISTRIBUTOR or to a reputable laboratory with lab access letter, all the items set forth below.

## I. PICTURE ITEMS

1. Original Picture Negative.

2. Soundtrack Negative.

3. Answer Print

4. Videotape Master: a videotape master of the original motion picture and television version thereof.

5. M & E Track: the music track and the effects track on separate channels.

6. Sound Tracks: separate dialogue tracks, sound effects tracks, and music tracks.

7. Complete Materials to Create Trailer.

## II. DOCUMENTATION

1. Continuity Script: two copies of the dialogue cutting continuity (in English), being an accurate transcript of dialogue, narration and song vocals.

2. Title Sheets: one typewritten list of all words appearing visually in the Picture suitable for use in translating such words into another language.

3. Music Cue Sheets: two copies of a music cue sheet showing the particulars of all music contained in the Picture, including the sound equipment used, the title of each composition, names of composers, publishers, and copyright owners.

4. Copyright Information: information as to the copyright proprietor(s) of the Picture, as well as copies of all copyright registrations, assignments of copyrights, and/or copyright licenses in Producer's possession (or in the possession of Producer's agents or attorney).

5. Chain of Title: copies of all certificates of authorship. Licenses, contracts, assignments and the written permissions from the proper parties interest, establishing Producer's "Chain of Title" with respect to the Picture and all elements thereof and permitting Producer, and its assigns to use any musical, literary, dramatic and other material of whatever nature used by Producer in the Production of the Picture.

6. Screen Credit Obligations: a copy of the screen credit obligations: for all individuals and entities affiliated with the Picture

7. Color Slides: at least 20 color slides (35 MM color transparencies) and any available prints of black and white still photographs and accompanying negatives, and at least 20 color still photographs and accompanying negatives depicting different scenes from the Picture, production

activities, and informal poses, the majority of which depict the principle members of the cast.

8. Website materials: artwork, text, bios and any other background material needed by DISTRIBUTOR to market the Picture on its website.

9. Shooting Script

10. Copyright Certificate: two U.S. Copyrights (Stamped by the library of Congress). If the copyright application has not yet been received from the Library of Congress, then Producer shall deliver a copy of the Application PA form, along with a copy of the cover letter and two (2) copies of the Copyright Certificate to DISTRIBUTOR when received from the Library of Congress. If application has not been made DISTRIBUTOR shall apply for the U.S. copyright at Producers expense.

## PRODUCER'S REPRESENTATIVE

A producer representative, or "producer rep," is a marketing and distribution consultant to the producer. A good producer rep is the "Jerry McGuire" of the film distribution industry. This guy knows everybody. He's got executives on speed dial. Knows who's who. And isn't afraid to go out there and use his relationships to get distribution for your film. You're more than happy to part with his commission.

Hold on to the commission if you already have your own contacts, know which distributor is best for your film and are confident of your negotiating skills. If that is the case, there's no need for a producer rep. Go out there and make the deal yourself.

If that's not the case, however, and you've already tried to find distribution on your own but no one's knocking at your door, hiring a specialized agent might be your most viable option.

A good producer rep will devise a powerful strategy to expose your film in the best possible light. If it has a shot at winning awards at major film festivals, he will be there to create a strong buzz. Otherwise, he will leverage his years of experience to call up the right distributors directly and arrange screenings. Above all, he will always try to stir competition among buyers in order to attain the highest possible price for your film.

A producer rep secures either worldwide distribution, which includes U.S. and foreign territories, or strictly domestic in which case you will also need the services of a sales agent to take care of the foreign arm of the deal. In this section, we will discuss using a producer rep for domestic distribution.

Bear in mind, this isn't the actual distribution agreement. This is only the beginning. Once the contract between producer and rep has been signed, the rep will be free to go out there and solicit the best distribution deal on your behalf.

## PRODUCER REP AGREEMENT

Dear _____:

THIS AGREEMENT, effective as of _____, 20____ will confirm the agreement ("Agreement") the basic terms you, _____ ("Producer"), and _____ ("Representative") have agreed upon with regard to your motion picture entitled "_____" ("Project").

> **Introductory paragraph.** This paragraph should not be taken lightly because it contains the effective date which may subsequently control some of the terms of the contract. Since the parties rarely sign the agreement on the same day, it is important to establish the date right at the top rather than running the risk of having two different dates next to the signatory lines at the end of the contract.
>
> It also introduces both parties — the Producer and the Producer Representative — to the contract. It also states the film title.

1. **TERM**: This Agreement shall be for a term ("Term") of one (1) year from the date of its complete execution; provided, however, that in the event Representative is in good faith negotiations with a distributor to license the Project, this Agreement shall automatically be extended for a period of 90 days. Upon expiration of the initial Term, Producer may terminate the Agreement on written notice at any time. Until such time as Producer terminates, the Term will be automatically extended.

> **Term.** It deals with the length of time the producer rep has to sell your film.
>
> It can be discussed either in terms of one or more festivals or actual years.
>
> In the first sentence of this example, the time span is set at only one year. There's nothing wrong with that as long as you have the option to take your film elsewhere, if nothing happens during that period.
>
> Now, look at the last two sentences. Unless the producer provides written notice the term is extended.
>
> **\*Legal Secret\*** Although easy to miss, it's imperative to understand what is going on. It basically means that if you don't give the producer rep "written" notice at the end of the term, it will be automatically renewed tying up for your film for an extra year. A small detail can make a big difference. This is a prime

> example of seemingly innocuous language which needs to be
> properly revised before signing the contract.

2. **EXCLUSIVITY**: During the Term herein, Representative shall have the sole and exclusive right to perform those services set forth in Paragraph 3 below. Producer shall not circumvent or arrange for distribution of the Project except through Representative. Notwithstanding the foregoing, nothing in his paragraph shall restrict Producer's own efforts respecting the arranging for completion financing, distribution and exploitation of the Project; provided however that any such efforts shall be made in consultation with Representative, shall not involve any third party acting in the role of Representative, shall be subject to all other terms of this Agreement, and any transactions which arise out of Representative's efforts shall be subject to Representative's fee as set forth in Paragraph 4 below.

> **Exclusivity.** The second clause establishes that a producer can neither use other reps during the term of his contract nor attempt to make his own deals. If he wants to strike out on his own, he'd have to consult first with his rep who gets paid no matter what.
>
> For example, your rep takes the film to a festival where you garner an award but no distribution. Based on that and while still under contract, either another rep or a distributor directly gets in touch with you but despite being interested, they don't like dealing with your agent. If you end up reaching an agreement on your own, your original rep is still entitled to his fees even though he wasn't the one to negotiate it.

3. **SERVICES**: During the Term hereof, Representative shall utilize its good faith efforts to arrange distribution of the Project in all media throughout the world ("Territory") and in all

versions. Representative shall have the exclusive right to contact and deal with distribution and/or foreign sales companies/ entities with respect to the Project. Representative may also perform certain business affairs consultation services respecting distribution deals the fee for which shall be included in the fee for Representative's services set forth in Paragraph 4(a), below.

a) Representative shall draft, review, negotiate and comment on distribution agreements.

b) Notwithstanding any other provision contained within this Agreement, Producer shall have final approval over any and all financing/distribution agreement entered into with regard to the Project, which approval shall not be unreasonably withheld.

c) Producer understands, acknowledges, and agrees that Representative may represent other project makers in similar capacities.

d) Representative agrees to consult Producer at all reasonable times during negotiations.

---

**Services**. It deals with the type of services a producer rep is expected to provide when arranging distribution.

What's important about this clause is not so much what it states but rather what it purposely leaves out. Even the very first sentence of our example is suspect — "Representative shall utilize its good faith efforts to arrange distribution . . ." What do "good faith efforts" entail exactly? The rest of the clause doesn't get any more specific. Every producer rep prefers to keep it as vague as possible so they can't be held responsible for any single act at the end of the day.

---

> **\*Legal Secret\*** Know what your goal is before hiring a rep and make sure you're both on the same page. Come up with a strategy. Choose ahead of time which top film festivals you'd like to target. Decide on a plan A, and a plan B, and a C. If the first attempt doesn't pay off, a rep sometimes loses interest but you'd have already agreed on the next step. In this example, film festivals aren't even mentioned. Make sure you add your strategy to the contract.

4.  **CONSIDERATION**: For and in consideration of Representative's services, Representative shall be paid:

   a)  A flat fee of $_____against___% the gross revenues due Producer from the Project.

   b)  "Gross Revenues" are all sums due Producer from all Project distributors (or other buyers) from exploitation of the Project in any and all markets and media received by Producer at any time. Producer shall provide and pay for any promotional materials and expenses needed to market the Project.

The aforesaid __% contingency fee is not set by law and is negotiable between Representative and Client.

> **Consideration.** It deals with the appropriate remuneration of a producer rep which generally includes both a flat fee and a commission.
>
> The "flat fee" is paid upfront in one lump sum ranging anywhere from $2,500 to $15,000. In the absence of such an arrangement, the commission will be inevitably larger.
>
> The commission fluctuates between 5–15%. Obviously,

producers aspire to the low end and reps, the higher with a compromise often reached at 10%. If the upfront fee is elevated, the commission should be lower and vice versa.

Subsection (b) provides an intentionally oversimplified definition of "Gross Revenues."

**Legal Secret** Every rep would like the term "Gross Revenue" to include as much as possible — even money the distributor advances you for requested deliverables. You, on the other hand, should fight for the narrowest definition available — only for the actual sales of your film.

For example, if you needed an extra $100,000 to complete your film and you had inadvertently agreed to a rep's 15% without exclusions, they would actually be entitled to $15,000 of money you'd have otherwise recouped. Enough said.

5.  **EXPENSES**: Representative also shall be reimbursed for actual out-of-pocket costs and expenses incurred in connection with the Project including but not limited to local and long distance telephone calls, messenger and courier fees, postage, photocopying, faxes, parking, festival entrance fees, screening room rentals, shipping of prints, and similar items, if any. No single expense in excess of Two-Hundred dollars ($200.00) shall be incurred without Producer's prior consent. Representative may require prepayment of expenses. Producer shall receive periodic billing statements for services and expenses.

**Expenses.** It deals with distribution expenses and can also prove tricky. Once again, two plus may very well not equal four at all.

Let's suppose your rep is taking a total of five films to Sundance which requires one flat entrance fee of $1,000 per rep. An unscrupulous agent might try to charge that amount for each one of his films whereas, in reality, you should only be paying him $200.

> **\*Legal Secret\*** Producers should make sure festival entrance fees are pro-rated among all films the producer rep is "taking" to the festival (or market). You should also make sure you use caps to control the total mount of expenses incurred.

6. **CREDIT**: If credits on the negative of the Project have not been set, or the Project is re-cut, Producer will add a credit in the Project, substantially as follows: "NAME OF PRODUCER REPRESENTATIVE."

> **Credit.** Producer Reps often negotiate for credit. That's not a problem as long as the film isn't already "locked" when you hire him and his name appears solely in the closing credits.

7. **EXTENSION OF TERM/CONTRACTS**: Notwithstanding the expiration of the Term as defined herein, should Producer enter into an agreement with any company, entity or person that Representative has contacted regarding the Project during the Term hereof, for the period of two (2) years after the expiration of the Term, Representative shall be entitled to its consideration as set forth in Paragraph 4.

> **Extension of Term.** It deals with what happens after the term expires.
>
> Suppose a distributor who's been in negotiations with a rep decides to enter into a deal with the producer only after that rep is no longer involved with the film.
>
> In this example, the rep's entitled to his whole commission for up to two years following the expiration of the term since he was the one to have introduced the parties in the first place.

> **\*Legal Secret\*** Always attempt to lower the commission and shorten the extension period from two years to one. Otherwise, your original rep may get his 15% and a potential new rep another 15% and that's without counting the 20% distribution fee. Before you know it, you've already pledged a staggering 50% and you still need to pay all other fees and expenses. You may never see a dime or it will be a long time coming indeed.

8. **PAYMENTS**: Producer agrees that Representative shall receive all revenues due Producer from Distributors or licensees.

> **Payments.** Once the film turns a profit, who does the distributor send the first check to?
>
> In this instance, if your rep is the Jerry Maguire of the distribution world, you should be Cuba Gooding Jr. demanding to "Show me the money!"
>
> According to clause 8, he's usually the one to receive it.
>
> **\*Legal Secret\*** Always negotiate that the rep is obligated to forward you the check upon arrival. You don't want anyone sitting on your money indefinitely.

9. **DISCLAIMER OF GUARANTEE**: Nothing in this Agreement and nothing in Representative's statements to Producer will be construed as a promise or guarantee about the outcome or the results of Representative's services hereunder. Producer understands and acknowledges that the motion picture business is risky, unpredictable, and subject to cultural trends and the whims and personal tastes of Project buyers. Producer acknowledges that Representative makes no such promises or guarantees as to the results of his services hereunder. Representative's comments

about the outcome or the results of Representative's services hereunder are expressions of opinion only.

---

**Disclaimer of Guarantee.** The so-called "CYA" clause actually protects your Jerry Maguire in case he overstates his connections. Reps are used to namedropping companies you'd love to sign with such as Lionsgate, Summit or Fox Searchlight. Basically, this little disclaimer shields them from ever having to deliver.

Always be weary of inflated promises of distribution. Film is a risky business. There are no guarantees.

---

**10. ARBITRATION AND JURISDICTION:** Any controversy or claim arising out of or in relation to this Agreement or the validity, construction or performance of this Agreement, or the breach thereof, shall be resolved by arbitration in accordance with the rules and procedures of the Independent Film & Television Alliance (IFTA), said rules may be amended from time to time with rights of discovery if requested by the arbitrator. Such rules and procedures are incorporated and made a part of this Agreement by reference.

---

Arbitration. This is especially important for independent producers. Always add an arbitration clause to the contract. Instead of dragging a dispute through court which could take years to litigate and incur astronomical legal fees, it's in both parties best interest to have agreed in advance to arbitration. If you're unable to resolve the matter, this is the fastest and cheapest way to have it settled. I strongly recommend using IFTA because all of their arbitrators are attorneys who specialize in independent films.

---

Paragraph headings in this Agreement are used for convenience only and will not be used to interpret or construe the provisions of this Agreement.

IN WITNESS WHEREOF, the parties have executed this agreement as of the date hereof.

Please indicate your agreement with the foregoing by executing this letter in the space provided below and returning same to my office.

Very truly yours,

_____
NAME OF PRODUCER REPRESENTATIVE

Date: _____

READ, APPROVED AND ACCEPTED:

_____
NAME OF PRODUCER

Date: _____

## SALES AGENTS

Sales agents specialize in selling and licensing film projects throughout the world. They are your Jerry Maguires of the foreign film territories. They spend years cultivating relationships with distributors around the world. They attend international film markets, from the three major — Cannes Film Market (MIF), American Film Market (AFM) and European Film Market (EFM) — to the minor ones. They're familiar with the business landscape and language of each country. They know its currency, the exchange rate, what the best distribution channels are and how to collect your money.

In this section, we will take a look at what every producer needs to know to successfully negotiate such an agreement. Confusingly, sales agents are often referred to as "distributors" in this type of contract even though their role is strictly that of a middleman. Therefore, you end up paying not one but two commissions — one to the sales agent and one to the actual distributor. Let's assume you've completed your film, you've already secured U.S. distribution and you're about to negotiate your deal with the sales agent to launch into the rest of the world.


## SALES AGENT AGREEMENT


Dear _____:


This letter agreement made and entered into as of _____, 2010 sets forth the basic terms by and between you _____ ("Producer"), and _____ ("Sales Agent" (*aka "Distributor"*)). In consideration of respective covenants, warranties and representations, together with other good and valuable consideration, Producer and Sales Agent hereby agree as follow:

> **Introductory paragraph.** This paragraph should not be taken lightly because it contains the effective date which may subsequently control some of the terms of the contract. Since the parties rarely sign the agreement on the same day, it is important to establish the date right at the top rather than running the risk of having two different dates next to the signatory lines at the end of the contract.
>
> It also introduces both parties — the Producer and the Sales Agent — to the contract.
>
> Usually referred to as "distributor" in most contracts, he's still called a sales agent in this example for the sake of clarity.

1. **PICTURE**: Producer will deliver to Sales Agent the documentation, advertising and physical materials set forth in the attached Delivery Requirements (EXHIBIT A), relating to the motion picture, currently entitled "_____" (the "Picture").

> **Picture.** This clause may appear short and straightforward but it's really not. While it's obvious that it states the film title, it also happens to be laden with potential problems.
>
> A film isn't considered properly "delivered" until all documentation, advertising and physical materials are in the sales agent's possession. Ah, there's the potential problem!
>
> For the delivery requirement to be fulfilled, every last one of the items listed in Exhibit A at the end of this chapter must be first furnished along with the film. And that's only a shortened version of material usually expected.
>
> Many new filmmakers are under the false impression that simply sending the film to the distributor does the trick. It doesn't. If it's not properly "delivered", the sales agent isn't required to find distribution.

2. **TERRITORY**: The territory (herein "Territory") for which rights are granted to Sales Agent consists of the World (in all languages and in all formats) with the exception of the United

States, its territories, possessions & military bases, and English-speaking Canada.

> **Territory.** The territory is comprised of countries in which a sales agent has the right to exploit your film. They often seek worldwide control.
>
> **Worldwide** denotes the rights to distribute the film in any territory in the world, both foreign and domestic.
>
> **Domestic** usually means the U.S. and either English speaking or all of Canada. It may also include "U.S. territories, possessions and military bases."
>
> **Foreign** rights signify the rest of the world.
>
> **\*Legal Secret\*** It's generally in the producer's best interest to retain U.S. distribution according only foreign rights to a sales agent. Otherwise, they'd be entitled to take a fee and commission for a deal you could have probably made on your own with the help of an entertainment attorney.
>
> Clause 2 of our example specifies the agreement excludes both the U.S. and English-speaking Canada.

3. **TERM**: Five (5) years following the date of the full and complete delivery of all delivery materials set forth in the Delivery Schedule for Sales Agent's exploitation of the Picture in the Territory ("Term"). All licensing and/or distribution agreements which Sales Agent enters into on behalf of Producer shall not have licensing periods which exceed the Term without the prior written consent in each case by Producer.

> **Term.** It's the length of time a sales agent has to license your film.
>
> Sales agents generally want the longest term possible. They reason that they need their deal with you to be at least as long as the deal with distributor and they say it takes the distributor a long time to recoup their costs.

*Legal Secret* Long terms are definitely not in your best interest. Try not to give in because distributors will either recoup early or they won't at all. You should counter with a 2 year term so if you're unhappy you can walk away from the deal sooner rather than later. Or, you can simply renew your contract for a longer term, if all goes well.

In this example, the parties have settled for 5 years.

4. **EXCLUSIVE GRANT OF RIGHTS**. Producer hereby grants exclusively to Sales Agent, throughout the Territory and during the Distribution Term all the necessary rights for Sales Agent to manufacture, promote, market and sell, and otherwise exploit the Picture in any or all of the Formats by any means determined by Sales Agent in its sole discretion All rights not specifically granted to Sales Agent hereunder are expressly reserved by Producer.

**Exclusive Grant of Rights.** It refers to the rights a producer grants a sales agent to be able to exploit the film, including those to manufacture, promote, market, license and sell to distributors.

It also allows the sales agent to do so in any or all Formats, including Theatrical release, Video on Demand (VOD) on both cable and the internet, Home video (DVD), Pay and Network Television, Syndication as well as Digital.

Sales agents set up their booths in film markets throughout the year hoping to attract foreign distributors. All day long they take meetings in an effort to negotiate the so-called short form of the agreement which establishes the basic deal points of how much, how long and which specific film rights. If all goes well, a long form containing additional clauses will be drafted later on as the more formal version.

5. **ALLOCATION OF GROSS RECEIPTS**: "Gross Receipts" shall be defined as the sum on a continuous basis of all monies or other consideration of any kind received by, used by, or credited

to Sale Agent, Producer or the Picture from the lease, license, sales, rental, distribution, exhibition, performance, exploitation, or other exercise of each right in the Pictures, all without any deductions; throughout the term (and any renewals thereof) of each Distribution License Agreement secured by Sales Agent on behalf of Producer.

a. **Sales Agent's Fee** (*aka Distributor's Fee*): Twenty-five percent "off the top" ("Sales Agent's Fee") of all Gross receipts.

b. **Producer's Share of Remaining Gross Receipts**: From first Gross Receipts, Sales Agent shall deduct and retain a sum which equals the Sales Agent's Fee, and then Sales Agent's Expenses (see definition below). Thereafter, from all remaining Gross Receipts, seventy-five percent (75%) thereof shall be paid to Producer ("Producer's Share of Gross Receipts") and twenty-five percent (25%) thereof shall be paid to Sales Agent.

---

**Allocation of Gross Receipts.** It determines how much money each party makes and what position they're in when money starts coming in.

"Gross Receipts" consists of the total amount earned from film sales to various distributors.

In subsection (a) of our example, the sales agent is entitled to 25% of gross receipts "off the top" of each sale which means he's the first one to get paid. These fees vary between 20–30%.

In subsection (b), the producer also gets his share but not until the sales agent has recouped all expenses.

So in a 100K sale, the sales agent would take 25K right "off the top" and assuming expenses of 30K, there should be 45K left for the producer, right? Unfortunately, it's not that simple and the seemingly innocuous language of clause 5 (b) is to blame.

---

> **\*Legal Secret\*** In essence, the sales agent is attempting to get paid twice! Besides their 25% off the top of gross receipts along with expenses, they're also vying for an additional 25% off your net proceeds. This is why you should always have a qualified attorney review your contracts. Hidden traps may be set up throughout.

6. **SALES AGENT'S EXPENSES** (*aka Distributor's Expenses*): Sales Agent shall expend and recoup from "Producer's Share of Gross Receipts," all of Sales Agent's out-of-pocket servicing, marketing, publicity, promotion, delivery, distribution and any other customary expenses paid or incurred by Sales Agent in connection with the Picture (including, without limitation, all costs of the marketing and advertising campaign for Picture) ("Sales Agent's Expenses"), Sales Agent's Expenses shall not exceed the sum of Fifty Thousand Dollars (U.S. $50,000) without the prior written approval of Producer.

> **Sales Agent's Expenses.** It deals with the amount of money a sales agent has to spend selling your film. It also makes explicit they are able to recoup all costs before a producer gets paid.
>
> You should be aware, however, that sales agents have an unfortunate reputation for inflating expenses, as is the case in the first half of this clause. The best way around that is to have them agree to a cap of 30–60K depending on the type of film. Once they go above it, they would need your approval to keep spending.

7. **ACCOUNTING AND AUDIT RIGHTS**: Sales Agent shall render written statements yearly. All statements shall be sent not later than forty-five (45) days after the end of the respective accounting period and shall be accompanied by all monies due Producer. Sales Agent shall keep complete and accurate books and records at Sales Agent's corporate offices with respect to

Gross Receipts, Sale Agent's Expenses and Producer's Share of Gross Receipts. Sales Agent agrees that Producer may, once during each one (1) year period, but only once with respect to any particular accounting statement rendered hereunder, audit Distributor's books and records at Distributor's corporate offices only. In the event that an audit reveals a discrepancy of five percent (5%) or more, Distributor shall reimburse Producer the reasonable costs of such audit.

---

**Accounting and Audit Rights.** It establishes a sales agent's duty to account for all revenue generated by the film to the producer.

Sales agents usually prefer yearly accounting which means they would be required to send you an accounting report as well as a check only once a year. Not good news for the producer.

Quarterly reports should be the goal so that you can keep effective tabs on them four times rather than merely once a year. The most frequent compromise, however, is every six months.

The audit part of this clause refers to a producer's right to periodically review the sales agent's books to make sure everything remains above board.

---

8. **DELIVERY**: Producer hereby agrees to deliver to Sales Agent all of the Elements specified in Exhibit A hereto. Preparation and delivery of the Elements will be at Producer's expense. All costs associated with the use of the Elements, except as expressly provided in this Agreement, as well as the cost of delivery of the Elements back to Producer will be at Sales Agent's expense. Producer hereby understands, acknowledges and agrees that all Elements delivered to Sales Agent shall be pre-approved for Sales Agent's use and further understands, acknowledges and agrees that it will bear any costs and expenses incurred by Sales Agent if Sales Agent deems any such pre-approved Elements unacceptable following Sales Agent's receipt of said Elements.

**Delivery.** Sales agent agreements always list detailed technical specifications a producer has to provide in order to meet delivery requirements.

**\*Legal Secret\*** Make sure before you sign on the dotted line that you'll be able to deliver on time which usually means only thirty days later. Sales agents are notorious for refusing payment because of minor details. You should first comb the list of requirements for anything you might not have and can't get or afford and negotiate to either have it removed entirely or for additional time or money to help you cover the costs.

9. **DEFAULT**: In the event either party should violate any of the material terms and conditions of this Agreement and such default will remain uncured for a period of thirty (30) days after written notice has been delivered to the defaulting party, then in such event the other party will have the right to terminate all or any part of this Agreement by delivering written notice to the defaulting party of its intention to terminate. In the event Producer is in breach of the representations and warranties, Sales Agent will have the right to immediately terminate this Agreement and Producer will be required to immediately reimburse Sales Agent for any unrecouped Advance and all of its actual out-of-pocked costs and expenses incurred in connection with the Picture.

**Default.** If either party breaches the terms of the contract, the other party has a right to terminate it.

In reality, sales agents will attempt to severely restrict the producer's chances of ever walking away from the agreement as well as the type of remedies available to him.

The first half of clause 9 in this example contains ideal language for the producer but chances of actually getting it are slim to none. In fact, the second half is much more likely.

10. **ARBITRATION AND JURISDICTION**: Any controversy or claim arising out of or in relation to this Agreement or the validity, construction or performance of this Agreement, or the breach thereof, shall be resolved by arbitration in accordance with the rules and procedures of the Independent Film & Television Alliance (IFTA), said rules may be amended from time to time with rights of discovery if requested by the arbitrator. Such rules and procedures are incorporated and made a part of this Agreement by reference.

> **Arbitration.** This is especially important for independent producers. Always add an arbitration clause to the contract. Instead of dragging a dispute through court which could take years to litigate and incur astronomical legal fees, it's in both parties best interest to have agreed in advance to arbitration. If you're unable to resolve the matter, this is the fastest and cheapest way to have it settled. I strongly recommend using IFTA because all of their arbitrators are attorneys who specialize in independent films.

IN WITNESS WHEREOF, the parties hereto have executed this Agreement as of the date first written above.


[PRODUCER]


_____


[SALES AGENT]


_____

# EXHIBIT "A"
## DELIVERY REQUIREMENTS

Delivery of the Picture shall consist of Producer making delivery, at Producer's expense, to Sales Agent all the items set forth below.

## I.  PICTURE ITEMS

1.  Original Picture Negative.

2.  Soundtrack Negative.

3.  Answer Print.

4.  Videotape Master: a videotape master of the original motion picture and television version thereof.

5.  M & E Track: the music track and the effects track on separate channels.

6.  Complete Materials to Create Trailer.

7.  EPK — electric press kit.

8.  Key Art — poster art and logo.

## II. DOCUMENTATION

1.  Continuity Script: two copies of the dialogue cutting continuity (in English), being an accurate transcript of dialogue, narration and song vocals.

2.  Title Sheets: one typewritten list of all words appearing visually in the Picture suitable for use in translating such words into another language.

3.  Music Cue Sheets: two copies of a music cue sheet showing the particulars of all music contained in the Picture, including the sound equipment used, the title of each composition, names of composers, publishers, and copyright owners.

4.  Copyright Information: information as to the copyright proprietor(s) of the Picture, as well as copies of all copyright registrations, assignments of copyrights, and/or copyright licenses in Producer's possession (or in the possession of Producer's agents or attorney).

5.  Chain of Title: copies of all certificates of authorship. Licenses, contracts, assignments and the written permissions from the proper parties interest, establishing Producer's "Chain of Title" with respect to the Picture and all elements thereof and permitting Producer, and its assigns to use any musical, literary, dramatic and other material of whatever nature used by Producer in the Production of the Picture.

6.  Screen Credit Obligations: a copy of the screen credit obligations: for all individuals and entities affiliated with the Picture.

7.  Color Slides: at least 20 color slides (35 MM color transparencies) and any available prints of black and white still photographs and accompanying negatives, and at least 20 color still photographs and accompanying negatives depicting different scenes from the Picture, production

activities, and informal poses, the majority of which depict the principle members of the cast.

8. Website materials: artwork, text, bios and any other background material needed by DISTRIBUTOR to market the Picture on its website.

9. Shooting Script

10. Copyright Certificate: two U.S. Copyrights (Stamped by the library of Congress). If the copyright application has not yet been received from the Library of Congress, then Producer shall deliver a copy of the Application PA form, along with a copy of the cover letter and two (2) copies of the Copyright Certificate to DISTRIBUTOR when received from the Library of Congress. If application has not been made DISTRIBUTOR shall apply for the U.S. copyright at Producers expense.

11. E&O Insurance — (U.S. distribution)

## SELF-DISTRIBUTION — SPLITTING THE RIGHTS

At the end of the day, only a small percentage of independent films ever obtain U.S. theatrical distribution. It's a sad truth. With the aid of today's technology, however, dedicated filmmakers have a variety of self-distribution tools at their disposal so that they can promote and sell their movie directly to audiences.

We've already discussed securing domestic distribution either on your own or by employing a producer rep and foreign distribution with the help of a sales agent. Let's see what happens whether you've always wanted to strike it out on your own or you've already exhausted all traditional avenues. In an ideal scenario, you want to split up your rights among separate distributor deals — a theatrical release, VOD, DVD, television and, finally, a foreign sales agent agreement.

The following agreements highlight only some of the major deal points. In the complicated world of distribution, one sentence and often a single word can make a huge difference so it's always best to allow an experienced entertainment attorney to represent you.

## THEATRICAL SELF-DISTRIBUTION

In the case of Theatrical Self-distribution, you initially show your film in only one or a select few theaters to generate enough buzz to allow you to gradually expand to more theaters. Your ultimate goal with the so-called platform release is two-fold. Either attract the attention of a big time distributor who's willing to buy your film and give it much wider exposure; or garner favorable reviews which you can then use yourself as a powerful marketing tool to drive ancillary markets.

If you're thinking of going that route, you need to decide first whether you want to organize the theatrical release on your own or hire a Company to do it for you.

### Four Walling

"Four Walling" is when you decide to rent a theater out by yourself to screen your film. Depending on the venue, it can cost between $500–5,000 or even more per night. The good news is that you get to keep 100% of all ticket sales. And you have the opportunity to sell as much merchandise as you want at the screening.

If you haven't been accepted to any film festivals, Four Walling is a good way of generating reviews.

It's all up to you, however. You're the one calling the theaters to book your film, you're coordinating the marketing and getting in touch with the press and, finally, you're responsible for collecting all revenue.

## Service Deals

If all that sounds like a lot, your next option is a Service Deal. In this case, you hire an independent company to arrange theatrical distribution for you in much the same way a traditional distributor would. They're in charge of booking your film, handling marketing, calling the press and collecting all revenue on your behalf.

You must have planned ahead of time for this kind of scenario though. At around $50,000 per theatre, it needs to be budgeted. This amount would cover the service company's upfront fee as well as all distribution costs including marketing and advertising. Still, most companies require a minimum of 5 theatres so you're looking at a total cost of $250,000.

It can be a risky proposition because what you get in the end is a 50-50 split of ticket sales with the theatre. You may not make enough to recoup your investment although some filmmakers have had great success this way in the past.

*My Big Fat Greek Wedding* is a famous example. The production budget was $5 million, the advertising cost $1 million and the producers paid the service company, IFC Films, a flat fee of $300K. The film went on to gross over $240 million in the US box office. In a traditional deal, the distributor would have taken 35% plus expenses after the 50-50 split with the theatres. Clearly, the producers were much better off paying a flat fee rather than 35% of all monies earned.

Marketing is the key to theatrical self-distribution. Take advantage of social media — use Facebook, Twitter and bloggers. Understand who your target audience is and generate excitement online before your actual opening. Get people talking and have your trailer embedded in their blog or site. All this is vital to ensure the future life of your film because awareness created by a theatrical release is what drives the ancillary markets (VOD, DVD, TV and Foreign Rights) further down the line.

## VOD—Video On Demand

In order to secure VOD distribution, producers use an aggregator who will act as a middleman. As an individual producer, you can neither directly approach an internet VOD operator like iTunes nor a cable VOD operator like Time Warner. In both instances, you must avail yourself of the services of an aggregator.

Aggregators know the business inside out and have already developed solid relationships. They'll get you onto platforms you'd never be able on your own. With over 100 cable operators in North America, the possibilities are endless.

The simplified version of a digital sales contract that follows gives filmmakers a glimpse of what they'll be dealing with when the time comes to sign a deal with an aggregator.

## DIGITAL SALES AGREEMENT
### (VOD Distribution Agreement)

This Agreement entered into as of _____, 20__ (the "Effective Date") between _____ (hereby known as "Producer") and VOD Aggregator (hereby known as "AGG") sets forth the terms of Producer's engagement of AGG as Producer's agent in connection with the licensing, distribution and promotion of the motion picture (in whole or in part) entitled "_____" (the "Picture") in the Digital Media, as follows:

> **Introduction.** This paragraph should not be taken lightly because it contains the effective date which establishes the beginning of the term. It also introduces both parties — the aggregator and the producer — to the contract and specifies that this is a licensing, distribution and promotion deal in Digital Media (VOD). And provides the film title.

1. **Producer Agreement:** Producer hereby appoints AGG to act as Producer's exclusive agent in connection with (i) the licensing, distribution and other exploitation of the Picture in the Digital Media throughout the Territory and for the Term, and (ii) the advertising and promotion of the Picture (the "Advertising Rights") in all media now known or hereafter devised. As Producer's agent and on Producer's behalf, AGG has the right to enter into licensing, distribution and other agreements with third parties for the exploitation of the Picture in the Digital Media ("Distribution Agreements") and for the Advertising Rights, on terms that AGG deems reasonable in its sole discretion.

> **Producer Agreement.** It contains the basic deal points a producer agrees to. Namely, he appoints the aggregator as his agent allowing him to enter into distribution deals with third parties to exploit the film in Digital Media.

2. **Aggregator Agreement:** AGG agrees to use good faith efforts to generate exposure for the Picture and to maximize revenue from the licensing, distribution and other exploitation of the Picture in the Digital Media; however, AGG makes no representations or warranties with respect to its ability to obtain Distribution Agreements or to generate any minimum amount of revenue.

> **Aggregator Agreement.** It contains the basic deal points an aggregator agrees to. Namely, to make a "good faith effort" to maximize the film's exposure and generate revenue. Although it's explicitly stated that there are no guarantees of obtaining distribution, the aggregator wouldn't have entered into an agreement with you unless he felt it might turn out to be profitable.

3. **Term:** The initial term shall be three years from the Effective Date with successive one year extensions unless either party issues notice, in writing, of its intent to cease such extensions at least sixty (60) days prior to the end of the then-current annual period. Any decision not to extend the Term shall be effective prospectively and shall not affect Distribution Agreements entered into by AGG, including without limitation AGG's right to receive its share of Gross Receipts attributable to Distribution Agreements.

> **Term.** It's the length of time an aggregator has to find a distributor. In this example, the term is for three years. Usually, terms run between one and three years. Here, either party may choose to terminate the agreement by written notice sixty days prior to expiration. In that case, any existing distributor deals continue to be honored, if there are profits both you and the aggregator will keep collecting revenue.

4. **Territory:** The Territory (herein "Territory') for which rights are granted to AGG shall be North America.

> **Territory.** The territory includes the countries where the aggregator has the right to exploit the film and is usually divided to domestic and foreign.
>
> **Domestic** usually refers to the U.S. and either English speaking or all of Canada.

**Foreign** rights signify the rest of the world.

Although the territory is often worldwide, in this example it's been limited to North America.

**\*Legal Secret\*** Your best strategy is to entrust your foreign rights to a sales agent. The vast majority of VOD aggregators only serve domestic territories directly and employ sub-aggregators for the rest of the world which means the producer ends up paying double fees.

That's not to imply you should never allow a U.S. aggregator to use sub-aggregators. You need to know your numbers in advance and be able to determine who handles exactly what. If a filmmaker believes the use of a sub-aggregator is beneficial in specific territories, he should make sure to first cap all aggregator fees and then go ahead and close the deal.

5. **Aggregator Fee:** Twenty-Five Percent (25%) of Gross Receipts. As used herein, "Gross Receipts" shall mean all non-refundable sums actually received by AGG from the licensing, distribution and exploitation of the Picture.

**Aggregator Fee.** It's the fee an aggregator charges for his services along with overhead (offices and facilities) and should not be confused with the distributor's compensation.

In this example, it's set at 25% of Gross Receipts which means the total amount of money the aggregator generates from the film. In effect, this is whatever's left after the distributors themselves first take their own cut from the original gross profits.

6. **Producer Share:** AGG shall pay to Producer One Hundred Percent (100%) of Net Receipts. As used herein, "Net Receipts" means "Gross Receipts" less deductions for the following: (i) the Aggregator Fee; (ii) actual, verifiable, third-party expenses incurred by AGG in connection with the marketing, promotion,

distribution, or other exploitation of the Picture, including without limitation encoding and delivery expenses; (iii) actual, verifiable, third-party collection and/or audit costs incurred by AGG in connection with review of third party licensees of the Picture; and (iv) any taxes, duties or other amounts payable by law in connection with the distribution of the Picture.

---

**Producer Share.** It's the amount of money that actually reaches the producer after all fees, expenses, checking costs, taxes and deductions have been taken off the top. In this example, it's set at 100% of net profits.

**\*Legal Secret\*** If that sounds too good to be true, it's because it is. All it really means is that you're getting 100% of whatever's left after both distributor and aggregator take their own cut. In essence, only 30% of net profits. Tricky, right?

---

7. **Digital Media:** "Digital Media" means all electronic and digital processes through which the Picture may be delivered for viewing, whether now known or hereafter devised, including without limitation as follows: (i) through all forms of Internet streaming, digital download, and electronic sell through; (ii) through all forms of video-on-demand, including without limitation via cable, satellite, Internet, "closed-IP" networks, IPTV, telco services, and wireless; (iii) through so called "disc on demand," "manufacture on demand," and similar fulfillment services; (iv) to mobile and handheld devices whether through wireless telephony and data networks or otherwise; (v) to hotels, educational institutions, libraries, and airlines and ships registered in and/or flying the U.S. flag in the Territory.

**Digital Media Outlets.** It refers to the various outlets an aggregator uses to exploit the film.

The two major Video On Demand platforms are Cable VOD and Internet VOD with Hotel VOD and Airline VOD, the remaining options.

**Cable VOD** includes your basic MSOs or cable "multiple system operators" which are cable providers like Comcast, Time Warner, Cablevision, Cox, Charter, etc. Cable VOD also includes "telco" companies like Verizon Fios and AT&T U-verse as well as satellite operators like Dish Network and DirecTV (who are really pay-per-view on their "linear" channels) and Mobile VOD.

**Internet VOD** includes Internet Rental where your movie's streamed on outlets like Best Buy's Cinema Now, Apple's iTunes, Amazon VOD, Microsoft's Xbox, Sony's Playstation, Nintendo Wii, Walmart's Vudu and Google's Google Play. All of these outlets also offer "electronic sell through" or EST which allows you to actually download and own the film at price points comparable to DVD sales.

8. **Editing:** AGG will not edit, and will not permit third parties to edit the Picture except for the following purposes: (i) to prepare closed captioned, subtitled and/or dubbed versions the Picture; (ii) to avoid legal liability or conform the Picture to applicable laws, standards and practices; (iii) to present the Picture in serial form without altering its linear form; (iv) to compress the Picture and/or the credits as required by any third party licensee in connection with time limitations in a manner then customary in the motion picture industry; and (v) to create advertising and publicity materials for the Picture

**Editing.** This is an important clause as it prevents the aggregator from interfering with the integrity of your film except to conform to different mediums.

9. **Delivery:** Producer shall deliver to AGG all of the required items set forth on EXHIBIT A (the "Essential Materials"). All necessary clearance, preparation, and delivery to AGG of Essential Materials shall be at Producer's sole cost and expense. Producer acknowledges and agrees that Producer's failure to timely deliver Essential Materials may prevent AGG from making the Picture available for distribution, and any delayed performance or non-performance by AGG arising from Producer's failure to meet its delivery obligations shall not be a breach hereof.

---

**Delivery.** It refers to all documents and other material a filmmaker is obligated to provide in order to satisfy the delivery requirements for his film.

Exhibit A at the end of the contract contains a short delivery list which varies depending on the type of picture produced among other factors. A 35MM motion picture, for example, doesn't have the same requirements as a digital one.

**\*Legal Secret\*** Besides the specific content of each list, what can also prove tricky is that some distributors still like to play games when it comes to the delivery clause, using technicalities as an excuse to refuse an advance or delay payment to the producer. So before you sign on the dotted line, you must make absolutely certain: 1) you have all the items, or 2) you can get all the items within the required time period, or 3) you've succeeded in having a particular item removed, or 4) you've convinced the Distributor to help you pay for what you need. Some items on the list are negotiable.

---

10. **Arbitration:** Any controversy or claim arising out of or in relation to this Agreement or the validity, construction or performance of this Agreement, or the breach thereof, shall be resolved by arbitration in accordance with the rules and procedures of the

Independent Film & Television Alliance (IFTA), said rules may be amended from time to time with rights of discovery if requested by the arbitrator. Such rules and procedures are incorporated and made a part of this Agreement by reference.

> **Arbitration.** This is especially important for independent producers. Always add an arbitration clause to the contract. Instead of dragging a dispute through court which could take years to litigate and incur astronomical legal fees, it's in both parties best interest to have agreed in advance to arbitration. If you're unable to resolve the matter, this is the fastest and cheapest way to have it settled. I strongly recommend using IFTA because all of their arbitrators are attorneys who specialize in independent films.

Paragraph headings in this Agreement are used for convenience only and will not be used to interpret or construe the provisions of this Agreement.

IN WITNESS WHEREOF, the parties have executed this agreement as of the date above.

AGGREGATOR:

_____

ACCEPTED AND AGREED:

_____

## EXHIBIT A
### Delivery List

**Video:**

1. One (1) copy of the Picture in high-quality HD or SD uncompressed format (Quick time preferred; 16:9 aspect ratio) on either data DVDs or external hard drive, or;

2. If the foregoing is not available, one (1) copy of the Picture on Digibeta or Beta SP.

3. Two (2) copies of the Picture on DVD;

4. A metadata form provided by AGG subsequent to execution of this Agreement, to be completed by Producer.

**Marketing & Promotional:**

5. (As available) any publicity slides or poster art in the rightful possession of Producer and fully cleared for use in connection with advertising and publicity related to the Picture provided as high-resolution digital files.

6. (As available) a trailer fully cleared for use in connection with advertising and publicity related to the Picture.

**Documentation:**

7. One (1) master music cue sheet specifying each musical composition contained in the Picture, and, with respect to each composition, the publisher, performer, composer and affiliated performing rights society.

8. Proof of Errors & Omissions liability insurance covering the Picture:
   a.  issued by an insurance carrier licensed in the Territory;
   b.  naming AGG, LLC as an additional insured;
   c.  with minimum limits of at least $1,000,000 for any claim arising out of a single occurrence and $3,000,000 for all claims in the aggregate with a deductible no more than $10,000;
   d.  coverage term must be at least three (3) year from the Effective Date.

9. Copies of the copyright certificate for the Picture (and, as applicable, the screenplay) in the United States, OR if a certificate is not available to Producer at the time of delivery, a copy of the copyright application (Form PA), accompanied by proof of payment of the copyright application fees.

**OPTIONAL ITEMS**

10. If available, bonus material (such as interviews with personnel, bloopers, deleted scenes, etc.) subject to the same representations and warranties regarding rights and clearances set forth in the attached Agreement and Schedule 1, and submitted in the formats described in #1 above.

11. If available, chain-of-title verification of Producer's rights in and to the Picture.

12. If available, copies of fully-executed agreements or deal memos for the writer, director, producer, composer and principal cast members of the Picture, as well as all other cast members, talent and personnel who are afforded credit on-screen in the main and end titles or the billing block, along with a key cast and crew contact list.

13. If available, copies of music publishing licenses, master use licenses and other rights and clearances for the Picture.

14. If available, a complete statement setting forth the names of all persons to whom Producer is contractually obligated to accord credit and/or likeness in any advertising, publicity or exploitation of the Picture.

## TELEVISION

Television consists of four principal outlets: pay-TV, basic cable, broadcast, and syndication.

Independent producers with a single movie generally use an aggregator for television deals who will act as a middleman. Similar to VOD deals, you can't approach many television outlets directly.

Aggregators know the business inside out and have already developed solid relationships. With an endless array of channels, the TV landscape is simply too vast for you to be able to accurately know where to take your film or what the going rates are for your film.

Television revenue has diminished considerably for independent films in recent years as networks increasingly either produce their own movies or have replaced them altogether with Reality TV.

## DVD — DIGITAL VIDEO DISC

In the case of a DVD deal, on the other hand, you can approach distributors directly with no need for an aggregator to act as middleman. All that's required is a good film and an experienced entertainment attorney.

The following contract outlines some of the major deal points of a standard DVD distribution agreement.

# DVD DISTRIBUTION AGREEMENT

This Agreement made and entered into as of _____, 20__, by and between _____ (hereby know as Distributor) and _____ (hereby known as Producer). In consideration of their respective covenants, warranties and representations, together with other good and valuable consideration, Distributor and Producer hereby agree as follows:

> **Introduction.** This paragraph should not be taken lightly because it contains the effective date which establishes the beginning of the term. It also introduces both parties — the distributor and the producer — to the contract.

1. **PICTURE:** Producer will deliver to Distributor the documentation, advertising and physical materials (the "Materials") set forth in the Delivery Schedule, relating to the motion picture with the running time of 85 minutes currently entitled: _____

> **Picture.** This clause may appear short and straightforward but it's really not. While it's obvious that it states the film title, it also happens to be laden with potential problems.
>
> A film isn't considered properly "delivered" until all documentation, advertising and physical materials are in the distributor's possession. Ah, there's the problem! Many new filmmakers are under the false impression that simply sending the film to the distributor does the trick. It doesn't. For the time being, all you need to remember is that if your film isn't properly "delivered", the distributor isn't required to do his part. And that means your film gets tied up indefinitely, no one will be able to see it and you won't get paid.

## 2. RIGHTS GRANTED:

a) Producer hereby grants to Distributor the irrevocable, right, title and interest in and to the distribution of the Picture, its sound, and music in the Territory (as hereinafter defined) including without limitation, the sole, exclusive, and irrevocable right and privilege, under Producer's copyright and otherwise, to distribute, license and otherwise exploit the Picture, its image, sound and music (as embodied in the Picture only), during the Term (as hereinafter defined) throughout the Territory (as hereinafter defined) for Home Video/DVD rights (the "Media").

b) Such rights do not include the rights to produce other motion pictures, or sequels, or remakes of the Picture or any right to produce television series, mini series, or programs or the rights to license clips from the Picture or other so-called ancillary rights (herein called "Reserved Rights").

---

**Rights Granted.** It refers to the rights a producer grants a distributor to exploit the film.

Pay close attention to the second to last line in the first paragraph. Here, the producer's granted the Distributor "home video/DVD" rights. It is imperative to comprehend the value of your media rights.

Understandably, if a DVD or VOD distributor offers an advance to license a recently completed film, an overeager producer will probably jump at the opportunity without fully grasping the ramifications of his actions. In fact, it is a grave mistake if you are interested in securing a theatrical distribution deal.

**\*Legal Secret\*** Domestic distributors know that many films actually lose money at the box office so they rarely take on the

---

> financial risk of a theatrical release without having also secured the potentially more profitable ancillary rights (DVD, VOD, internet media and television).

3. **RESERVED RIGHTS**: All other rights not expressly written herein, including but not limited to, theatrical, television, Video-on Demand (VOD), electronic publishing, print publication, music publishing, live-television, radio and dramatic rights are reserved to the Producer.

> **Reserved Rights.** These are the rights a filmmaker keeps for themselves so that he can either self-distribute or engage the services of another distribution company. Needless to say, it's important to understand exactly what's been retained so you can exploit these rights elsewhere.

4. **TERRITORY**: The Territory (herein "Territory") for which rights are granted to Distributor consists of the U.S. and english speaking Canada.

> **Territory.** The territory includes countries where a distributor has the right to exploit the film.
>
> Independent filmmakers often enter into more than one distribution deal in which case the rights are divided into two territories — domestic and foreign.
>
> **Domestic** usually means the U.S. and either English speaking or all of Canada. It may also include "U.S. territories, possessions and military bases."
>
> **Foreign** rights signify the rest of the world.
>
> In this example, it refers only to domestic.
>
> **\*Legal Secret\*** Your best strategy is to entrust your foreign rights to a sales agent. The vast majority of DVD distributors only

serve domestic territories directly and employ sub-distributors for the rest of the world which means the producer ends up paying double fees.

That's not to imply you should never allow a U.S. distributor to use sub-distributors. You need to know your numbers in advance and be able to determine who handles exactly what. If a filmmaker believes the use of a sub-distributor is beneficial in specific territories, he should make sure to first cap the distributor fees and then go ahead and close the deal.

5. **TERM**: The rights granted to Distributor under this Agreement will commence on the date of delivery to Distributor of all delivery items listed in Delivery Items, and continue thereafter for four (4) years ("Initial Term"). This Agreement will thereafter renew automatically for successive two (2) year periods (each, a "renewal Term"), unless either party notifies the other in writing at least thirty (30) days prior to the end of the Initial Term or any Renewal Term that it does not wish to renew. If such notification is given by either party, this Agreement will remain in full effect for a one (1) year "transition period" after the end of the then-current term to allow both parties time to make alternate arrangements. Exception: If Producer has not received at minimum $80,000 prior to the end of the fourth year (during the "Initial Term"), Producer may terminate this agreement by written notice to Distributor, 30 days prior to the fourth year anniversary of this contract.

**Term.** It's the length of time a distributor has to distribute the film.

DVD distributors are after long terms. Producers should only commit to shorter time periods, however, or based on the distributor's performance. The usual compromise is an initial short term with the option to extend, if the distributor pays a certain amount of money.

In this example, the contract provides for an initial term of four years. Upon expiration, either party may choose to terminate the agreement by giving written notice with an additional period of transition of one year. If possible, negotiate to have this last clause omitted.

**\*Legal Secret\*** Every producer should ask for a minimum payment, let's say at least $80,000, during the initial time frame. If the distributor is unable to meet this obligation then the term would automatically end in 30 days.

**6. ADVANCE/GUARANTEE**: There shall be no advance.

**Advance/Guarantee.** It's the money you receive up front for licensing your film to a distributor.

Under current market conditions, distributors are willing to offer advances only if a movie benefits from highly marketable elements like name actors, producers and/or director, or acceptance by a major film festival.

In this example, no such provisions are included.

**7. ALLOCATION OF GROSS RECEIPTS**: As to proceeds derived from Distributor's exploitation of all rights outlined in Paragraph 2, division of the Gross Receipts will be made, as follows:

a) From the Distributor's exploitation of Home Video/DVD, Distributor shall recoup all Recoupable Expenses (see paragraph 8).

b) From the remaining revenues, Distributor shall deduct and retain thirty (50%) of Gross Receipts.

c) The net proceeds shall be paid to Producer.

d) Gross Receipts: As used herein, the term "Gross Receipts" shall mean all monies actually received by and credited to Distributor less any refunds, returns, credit card/bank fees, taxes, collection costs, shipping & handling, and manufacturing or duplication costs.

e) Deductions from Gross Receipts shall be taken in the following order: 1) Recoupable Expenses incurred by Distributor. 2) Distribution fee of fifty percent (50%) of Gross Receipts 3) Net Proceeds shall be paid to Producer.

---

**Allocation of Gross Receipts.** Just a fancy way of saying who gets what in the end.

In this example, subsection (a) determines the distributor recoups all expenses off the top. In subsection (b), he also gets to take a fee of 50% "from the remaining revenue" of gross receipts for his time and effort. Finally, in subsection (c), the producer receives the remainder of what's called "net proceeds". Section (d) defines "Gross Receipts". While section (e) reviews once again the allocation of money.

**In the case of domestic home video/ DVD**, two basic formulas may be used. Either a 50/50 net or a royalty deal.

As in this example, a 50/50 net deal allows a distributor to deduct distribution expenses from the gross revenues and then split the balance 50/50 with the filmmaker.

A royalty deal, on the other hand, pays the filmmaker a royalty in the range of 20–25% of wholesale price for each DVD sold.

**\*Legal Secret\*** From the filmmaker's point of view, a royalty formula has the advantage of ensuring that you receive, at least, some revenue even if sales are minimal. Since your royalties are based on the specific number of units sold (minus returns) and supposed marketing expenses are irrelevant, there's less room for creative accounting.

**8. RECOUPABLE EXPENSES**: As used herein, the term expenses and/or recoupable expenses shall mean all of Distributor's actual expenses on behalf of the Picture limited as follows: a) DVD production and replication costs: These expenses include all direct out-of-pocket costs to produce and replicate professional standard DVDs, b) Promotional Expenses: These expenses include the cost of preparing artwork (e.g. DVD covers), posters, one sheets, trailers and advertising relating to the Picture. c) Delivery Expenses: Delivery Expenses are the direct out of pocket costs incurred by Distributor to manufacture any of the film, video or digital deliverables which Producer did not supply. Delivery Expenses also include the direct out of pocket costs incurred between markets for shipping, duplicating, and delivery of marketing materials (i.e. screeners), although Distributor will make best efforts to keep these low. At Producer's request, Distributor shall provide receipts for each and every expense. d) Recoupable Expenses do not include any of the Distributor's general office overhead but may include expenses tied directly to the management of Producer's materials (DVD inventory, fulfillment, communication).

---

**Recoupable Expenses.** It deals with the money a distributor has to spend in order to distribute your film.

This is where certain questionable accounting practices may come into play and two plus two doesn't always equal four.

You should always make sure your agreement clearly defines the type and amount of expenses the distributor is allowed to recoup.

Producers should negotiate to have a cap placed on all expenses as well as categorize them into distinct groups: 1) production and replication, 2) promotional and 3) delivery expenses.

In this example, subsection (a) deals with production and replication while subsection (b) deals with the costs of preparing

---

posters, one-sheets, trailers and advertising. The distributor should agree to a minimum amount of money to be spent (floor) as well as a maximum cap (ceiling). Finally, in subsection (c), Delivery Expenses cover the distributor's costs to manufacture all of the film deliverables.

You should always keep track of all distribution expenses because they will ultimately be deducted from your own revenue. If you fail to do so, it's money out of your own and your investors' pockets.

## 9. ACCOUNTINGS:

a) Distributor will render or cause to be rendered to Producer semiannual accounting statements showing expenses and receipts. Statements will be produced 15 days after the 30th of June and the 31st of December. Processing of these statements will begin 6 months after the signing of this Agreement and delivery of all Deliverables. All monies due and payable to Producer pursuant to this Agreement will be paid simultaneously with the rendering of such statements.

b) Distributor shall keep and maintain at its office, until expiration of the Term and for a period of three (3) years thereafter, complete detailed, permanent, true and accurate books of account and records relating to the distributing and exhibition of the Picture, including, but not limited to, detailed collections and sales by country and/or buyer, detailed billings thereon, detailed play dates if applicable thereof, detailed records of expenses that have been deducted from collections received from the exploitation of the Picture, and the whereabouts of prints, trailers, accessories and other material in connection with the Picture.

c) Producer shall be entitled to inspect such books and records of Distributor relating to the Picture during regular business hours and shall be entitled to audit such books and records of Distributor relating to the Picture upon ten (10) business days written notice to Distributor.

---

**Accounting and Audit Rights.** It establishes a distributor's duty to account for all revenue generated by the film to the producer.

DVD distributors usually prefer yearly accounting which means they would be required to send you an accounting report as well as a check only once a year. Not good news for the producer.

Quarterly reports should be your goal so that you can keep effective tabs on them four times rather than merely once a year. The most frequent compromise, however, is every six months.

---

20. **ARBITRATION:** Any controversy or claim arising out of or in relation to this Agreement or the validity, construction or performance of this Agreement, or the breach thereof, shall be resolved by arbitration in accordance with the rules and procedures of the Independent Film & Television Alliance (IFTA), said rules may be amended from time to time with rights of discovery if requested by the arbitrator. Such rules and procedures are incorporated and made a part of this Agreement by reference.

---

**Arbitration.** This is especially important for independent producers. Always add an arbitration clause to the contract. Instead of dragging a dispute through court which could take years to litigate and incur astronomical legal fees, it's in both parties best interest to have agreed in advance to arbitration. If you're unable to resolve the matter, this is the fastest and cheapest way to have it settled. I strongly recommend using IFTA because all of their arbitrators are attorneys who specialize in independent films.

---

Paragraph headings in this Agreement are used for convenience only and will not be used to interpret or construe the provisions of this Agreement.

IN WITNESS WHEREOF, the parties have executed this agreement as of the date hereof.

DISTRIBUTOR:

_____

ACCEPTED AND AGREED:

_____

www.ingramcontent.com/pod-product-compliance
Lightning Source LLC
Chambersburg PA
CBHW070400200326
41518CB00011B/2003